CLIMATE OF EXTREMES: Landscape and Imagination

by

Marilyn Stablein

Marilyn Stablein

BLACK HERON PRESS
SEATTLE, WASHINGTON

Published by
BLACK HERON PRESS
P.O. Box 95676
Seattle, Washington 98145

Cover Art by Deborah Mersky

ISBN: 0-930773-38-1 (Cloth)
0-930773-39-X (Paperback)

Typeset in Adobe Garamond at Dataprose
Printed in U.S.A.

ACKNOWLEDGMENTS

I am grateful to the editors and publishers who first brought into print the following essays: "Wet Babies" in ZYZZYVA; "After the Hurricane" and "Intrusions in Ice" in the anthology *The Truth About the Territory: Contemporary Nonfiction from the Northwest* (Owl Creek Press); "After the Hurricane" also appeared in the anthology *Hurricanes* (Black Heron Press); "Two Men From the Sea" under a different title in *The Beacon Review;* excerpts from "Deceptions in Gray" in the anthology *15: Seattle Book* and *The Literary Center Quarterly;* and "Deep in the Forests of Home" in *The Santa Clara Review.*

"Intrusions in Ice" with illustrations by M. Kasper was published by Wash n' Press, 1988.

CONTENTS

PREFACE
Landscapes of Impermanence

This collection has had a circuitous history. At first I called it my "Weather Book" because a number of the essays are about weather; gray misty days in Seattle, the aftermath of a Texas hurricane, ice falls and windstorms. There are no sunny beach scenes, few calm skies and clear waters here. Rather I write about weather that makes me stand up and take note, not lie back and go to sleep, charismatic weather that may herald the advent of disaster.

Sometimes I wonder if my curiosity about disaster stems from where I grew up, not far from the fog-shrouded turbulent Pacific, in the earthquake-prone flatlands of California. A land accosted by a daily threat of disruptive weather, where a perpetual season of golden sunny afternoons and star-filled nights is undermined by the shaky ground and the natural scarcity of fresh water.

Like South Sea islanders who routinely face the threat of seasonal hurricanes, we Westerners acclimatize to the vagaries of our own wild weather, the apocalyptic vibrations of the ground and land slipping into the sea, the eruptions of fire and lava, the dramatic circulations of winds that stir up firestorms and tidal waves. With our omnipresent threat of disaster, we learn to sublimate, relegate fear to a dark region of the unconscious until disaster strikes; then fear bursts out in a turmoil of panic and confusion.

I think of earthquakes as a type of weather since they occur unpredictably, and are external intrusions of the physical world. Earthquakes in the West, though defined as catastrophic events, are actually common and familiar. Students in elementary school practice taking cover during an earthquake; supermarket grocery bags are imprinted with emergency earthquake instructions and public libraries carry pamphlets of tips on survival after an earthquake. Etched in our communal mind's eye are vivid television images from recent earthquakes: freeways collapsing on top of automobiles, flattening cars and drivers underneath a mound of rubble; the upper deck of the Oakland Bay bridge caving in midspan over the choppy waters of San Francisco Bay; and every type of shaken, tumbled and flattened building from city high-risers to antique Victorians in rural California.

Near the geysers of Calistoga, geothermal plants and hot-spring vents surround the ridges and canyons, and earthquakes erupt in clusters or swarms. To the east volcanoes punctuate the Sierra skyline. Most are dormant; their silhouettes rise on the horizon, vivid reminders of eruptions of the past. On Alki Beach in Seattle one afternoon, I saw the steam-and-ash cloud rise from Mount St. Helen's eruption, over a hundred miles south. Such visions, those fiery and sooty spectacles, dramatically undermine lazy days at the beach.

Offshore to the west, the ocean covers the greatest concentration of active volcanoes on earth. I will never see the eleven hundred seamounts and volcanic cones, some of which rise seven thousand feet from the ocean floor, but I feel their presence. In deep underwater vents, giant sea worms and plants unique to that strange environment, plants that do not need sun, thrive in the boiling temperatures.

The Far West is a region of intimidation. The potential for destruction both tempers and unnerves, consciously and subconsciously, those who live there. The Oakland-Berkeley Hills firestorm came within a half mile of my house. While the fire didn't destroy my home, I felt the displacement of evacuation and mourned the loss of entire neighborhoods and ecosystems. If Westerners are edgy, it's with good cause. Disasters and mortality, survival and preparations are natural conditions and preoccupations.

Westerners are not the only ones who battle the elements. My first winter in upstate New York was the coldest I ever experienced and the coldest in the history of the region. While extreme winter weather conditions are unpleasant and difficult, winter is a predictable phenomenon, a seasonal occurrence. Low temperatures, snow and ice are typical winter elements and except for the usual spate of hazards and accidents, cold weather conditions are not life-threatening to large numbers of people. Severe snow and icefalls can knock out power lines, collapse roofs, and wreak havoc on the roads, but houses do not burn up, flatten or slide down seaside cliffs. Freeways may shut down for a day but overpasses do not collapse onto the roads, nor do gaping cracks fork pathways through pavement and cement. Endurance and common sense are the keys to survival. The snow always melts as spring creeps closer to summer. Meanwhile there are aesthetically pleasing vistas of white, elegant snowscapes and the incredible permutations of ice.

"Weather Book" was a short-lived title. Much as I am enthralled by catastrophic weather, I realize weather is only an agent of change. Weather is inseparable from the landscape it affects. There are landscapes of destruction, of earthquakes, tidal waves, hurricanes, and blizzards; and interior landscapes, the climate of closed spaces, the weather of dreams, memory and the imagination. Landscape has a way of slipping into the transforming consciousness. When fog slips into a coastal town and erases buildings, streets and woods, or when ice coats the branches and snow shrouds the ground, vistas of absence and dormancy cloud my mind.

Every change in the landscape follows a downward progression, that is, toward the demise of order and the disintegration of life and body. Landslides and avalanches signal crumbling mountains; hurricanes transform vacation beach homes into instant rubble. Disintegration inevitably points to destruction, decay and death. Whether I witness a catastrophic event or watch the tiniest dew drop dissolve on a window pane, the conditions are similar—all phenomena dissolve and disintegrate.

The more I think about change and watch the shift of seasons, the more I acknowledge the impermanence of all things. The notion of impermanence lies behind every creature's struggle for survival; the struggle to survive in the wild becomes a metaphor, the prototype for every possible struggle. The landscapes of my life, many located in the West, are catalysts for thinking about my place in the world, and how fragile and temporary human existence is and how fragile the natural environment is.

To offset the sobering truth of my own inevitable journey towards death, I take pleasure in noticing the changes of weather, the details of destruction. There is a beauty in the way the elements touch or move through a landscape. I never tire of watching the seasons manifest themselves. Visions of natural disasters enthrall me.

Impermanence is a constant, a universal truth. What in this world is permanent? Rocks, wildlife, earth, water, air, human life—all is in motion and flux. Impermanence is the root of change. The disintegration of the physical world points to the inevitable progress of death. In this sense, this collection is not about where I live and work, nor about the climate and landscapes of the North American continent. Rather these are somber vistas of impermanence. The wilder the weather, the harsher the climate, the greater my reveries of vulnerability. In the absence of shelter and permanence, all climates are extreme.

DEEP IN THE FORESTS OF HOME

I grew up in a quiet residential neighborhood not far from the bay, twenty-five miles south of San Francisco. The landscapes ranged from dry inland vegetation—cultivated cacti and palms—to flora that thrived with seasonal rains and a year-round heavy ocean dew. Patches of bamboo, ivy, and fern lined the well watered edges of shady patios. Thrusting up out of this confusion of dry and moist was a haphazard proliferation of the native redwood. The town was named Palo Alto, in fact, by Portola, an early Spanish explorer who slept under the "tall" (Spanish, *alto*) "stick" (Spanish, *palo*) of a redwood tree on his early travels up the coast. Today this namesake survives but is neither the tallest nor the healthiest specimen.

To the east behind a line of back yard fences, railway tracks carried trainloads of commuters into the city. Poisonous oleander bushes, dusty with train soot, and the steel tracks with oil-soaked redwood railway ties created a sinister boundary. "Stay off the tracks," Mother warned, "and don't eat any oleander leaves."

I squeezed through a picket fence to glimpse, at closer range, locomotives that thundered night and day just two blocks from home. Sometimes a friend and I lined up rocks and pennies on the tracks but our efforts did nothing to thwart the train's progress or transform the metal coins. The pennies always blew off before the huge metal wheels could flatten them. My whole body shook when a passing train lurched within a few feet of me. If I waved to the engineer in his cabin or to the conductor who smoked a pipe and leaned over the back railing of the caboose, I might elicit a wave back, a sign which legitimized, somehow, my forbidden presence.

To the west, parallel to the tracks, a steady stream of vehicles traveled the Camino Real. Beyond that, the Stanford foothills, grassy, rolling lumps of land, ascended gradually to the coastal range that separated the peninsula from the Pacific. When coastal fog spilled over the Santa Cruz Ridge and seeped down, swallowing the foothills and occasionally the neighborhood, I remembered the nearness of the great waters of the ocean. I imagined fog was the steamy, moist breath exhaled by the mermaids who rose up on the shore at night to rest and comb their long hair.

A high school rimmed the northern edge of the neighborhood and a park the eastern side. Each possessed huge expanses of lawn, playgrounds or playing fields with dugouts and bleachers, parking lots and groves of trees. There were dangers in these areas, too. At the park bullies and gangs roamed looking for victims. Once I was walking across a field at the school when I heard a whistle. When I looked, a man came out from behind the dugout and stood facing me, his pants a heap of cloth at his ankles. In his hand his penis waved violently back and forth. I raced for home and he hopped on a bike and sped away.

As long as I didn't step outside the boundaries, I was free to roam the neighborhood whose streets were named after California trees: Manzanita, Sequoia, Mariposa, Madrona. Fences didn't stop me. I knew the locations of wildly delicious forbidden fruits: nectarine, apricot, loquat, peach, orange, mulberry, walnut, almond, and Japanese and Santa Rosa plums. A pomegranate tree grew in a neighbor's yard. Amazingly those barren limbs produced the richest, sweetest ruby fruits, carefully hidden beneath an ugly brown outer peel, and a delicate white inner skin.

I learned the treacheries of wood: the throb of a splinter wedged into my skin; how my thigh burned after sliding down a fence too fast in shorts; how my feet pounded when I landed after dropping from a branch high above the ground.

Where the school bus dropped me, a lemon tree dangled over a back yard fence. I'd pick a lemon and suck on it as I walked home. Sometimes I sucked the juice out of a hole I bit through the skin. Even the peel had a savoriness that was both pungently bitter and exciting. My lips puckered from the acidic sting, though the pilfered lemons were sweeter than the grocery store lemons. Once I carefully peeled a thin-skinned lemon and ate the sections, one by one, pretending it was an orange. My teeth squeaked from the gritty juice.

I often perched in the twisted branches of the manzanita tree that grew at the side of our house. I liked to think that our tree was the inspiration after which our three-block-long street was named. When I rode my bike down to Peers Park, the playground to the south, I'd sit in my favorite eucalyptus tree. This tree had a thick trunk at the ground, but within climbing distance, the base spread out like fingers from a palm, into three separate trees. Enclosed in the nest of the tree, I watched softball games or peeled at the bark etched with my initials and tracked the ants which scurried upwards into the highest limbs.

Not every tree had fruits or seeds, but many did. Wrinkly, pink peppercorn-sized seeds from the pepper tree were an essential ingredient in mud pies and cakes. I collected pine cones at Christmas and sprayed them with a glittery silver paint. Around Thanksgiving I cut sprigs from the twin holly trees that stood on either side of our front walk. Father was allergic to the enormous, puffy, cream-white magnolia blossoms from the trees in the front parking strip, so I couldn't pick them for bouquets. But I kept the furry brown seed pods with bright red berries on my dresser top where I kept other seeds, pods and cones to string into necklaces or just to admire. Each day as I tended my altar to the spirits of the outdoors I examined and rearranged my natural found treasures.

The trees had their seasons and cycles. Not all of them survived into longevity. Trees that withered from a summer drought never revived in the spring when the other trees sent out fresh, green buds. Dead trees froze in a barren, perennial autumn. Some trees succumbed to the effects of violent weather or a vandal's saw. One night a row of sycamores lining the road to the high school was felled with a chain saw. All winter the ugly severed stumps were sore reminders of an unthinkable and dumb prank.

One violent storm uprooted trees and sent trunks, limbs and leaves crashing onto roofs, sidewalks and pavement. My parents blamed the jet stream which I envisioned as a fierce river of air high above our town, invisible yet erratic and loaded with rain. Later when I no longer heard the jet stream mentioned, I wondered if the theory had gone out of fashion or did the weather irreversibly change?

One night during a storm, the giant oak tree across the street keeled over. The thud and crack of snapping limbs shook the house. In the morning the sight reminded me, in an odd way, of the cowboy scene where a horse stumbles and breaks a leg—a sorry situation with only one dire solution: shoot the horse. I had never seen a fallen tree before, not a tree that was still alive. How did the wind become so strong? Why did the oak fall and not the sycamore or redwood?

The fallen oak blocked the street and we had to drive another way. If one fierce blow of air could push the tree over, I thought, why couldn't another strong blow from a crane, bulldozer or the enormous hand of God, upright the tree again. Every day I looked for signs of death, but the leaves still bristled, green and healthy. The city street crew came after three days. With chain saws they cut the trunk into pieces that fit in our fireplace. The men hauled smaller branches and leaves away in a large truck. Within two days, the tree had entirely disappeared. After that, when the kids on the block played hide-and-seek, we used another tree trunk to rest our heads against, as we closed our eyes tightly and counted to fifty. When we had fires that winter, I stared into the hot coals looking for signs of the oak, remembering the spot where the tree once stood.

Of all the trees in the neighborhood, the redwood was the most mysterious. A tree that defies seasons, whose longevity gives admirable stance against the forces of disintegration. Redwood earned the epithets: majestic and grand. Two grew in our back yard and shaded the house. The branches were so high up, they were impossible to reach or climb on. Falling needles and shedding bark covered the ground and few plants could grow underneath. The trees were so tall, when I stretched my neck and tilted my head back, I couldn't see the tops from the back yard.

One summer when my family camped at Big Basin I walked through groves of redwoods for the first time. Here the trees grew, reseeded, and thrived. Wind howled from an overhead corridor. The trees spoke in breezes that whistled and rustled hundreds of feet overhead. Trees pushed back the sky. I could see only a few blue patches through the lofty, sheltering branches. If rain fell, not many drops penetrated the pine needle-carpeted earth. When I walked in a wilderness of first-growth redwoods, I entered another country, the country of trees.

The woods rationed and screened the sun. The tallest branches filtered the sunlight, and only a few rays penetrated the thick foliage. This isolation of light, the parceling of brilliance into distinct beams, changed my awareness of light. Suddenly light became precious and rare. At summer camp, during sunset church services in a redwood grove, light pierced the immense outdoor sanctuary like beams through a stained glass window. Where light fell, beauty flickered.

I studied redwoods in school and came to appreciate their statistics. In a perspective of superlatives, redwood is the grandest, the Paul Bunyan of trees. In terms of height, redwoods are the tallest trees—not only in my neighborhood, but in every neighborhood throughout the world. A grove of redwoods is heavy with living matter: bark, pith, sap, root, branch, and needle. The sheer bulk of vegetation. A thick and weighty redwood may weigh two thousand tons. If I calculate the weight of vegetation per square foot, a redwood grove far outweighs all other environments.

Mature redwood trunks are thick. A car can drive through the hollowed-out trunk of a living redwood tree. I know because my father, on a vacation once, drove the family car through the trunk of a redwood tree in a resort in northern California. He paused the car under the great tree. We idled in park, beneath the towering giant, safe in the cavern of growth and life. I felt for a moment as if I had acquired some rare ability or gift like walking on water. I vaporized my body to walk through trees, through solid matter.

Redwoods are ancient. During the life span of a single redwood tree, history books record the rise and fall of entire civilizations. In a state park exhibit at a freeway rest area, I counted the tree rings. One huge slice of a redwood trunk was dotted with flags. The flags pinpointed famous events: the year World War I broke out, the year of the European plague, the year Columbus discovered America. The flag stuck in the ring marking the year of Christ's birth was set many rings away from the center of the trunk, many years after the first recorded year of the young sapling.

When I visit a redwood grove now, memories of childhood crowd into my mind. I'm as amazed now as I was when I first walked the forests of the West in the country of trees. When the force of the wind shakes the lofty branches, the way the silence breaks reminds me of the distant roar of the ocean I hear when I put my ear to a conch shell. The silence is special. Unlike the artificial closed-in silence of a closet or room, the silence of a vast space seems a mystical cooperation between countless forest creatures. When a leaf from one of the scattered deciduous trees falls and floats through the cavernous growth of evergreens, the slight crackling breaks the thick silence. In the weatherless stillness, the descent of a solitary leaf is a momentous and ghostly occurrence.

Landscape has a way of slipping into and transforming consciousness. The calm of the forest is other-worldly, beyond the upheavals of weird weather or the raucous congestion of cities. The forest is a type of panacea for turmoil and stress. As soon as I enter the deep, dark and still woods—the redwood forests are the deepest, darkest—I'm transported into another realm where depression and small-minded fears are removed. Rays of light spotlight patches of the dark. Incredibly, in those very spots where a thin ray does penetrate, plants vie for light that is so elusive, the beams only linger a few minutes each day.

When I was growing up, trees enclosed my neighborhood and defined my world. I no longer clamor to buy redwood curios for sale at highway stands: earrings, name tags, mugs, bowls, spoons, plaques, and large sculptures and chainsaw art of totems, eagles and Paul Bunyans. I no longer climb trees or pilfer fruit, and the landscapes that rim my horizons have expanded.

Yet I wonder if growing up in the midst of those great trees still affects the way I think. To acknowledge these inhabitants from a larger order of being is to recognize a presence greater than my physical being. When I compare my own growth, the length and height of my body, for instance, to that of a redwood, I find my physical presence doesn't measure up to much. My body will confront the inevitable disintegration of bone, marrow, gut and pulse, growing older, maturing, fruiting, and finally aging long before a redwood tree reaches maturity.

The natural spectacle of growth in the forests where the trees grow tall and wide is formidable. The statuesque redwood commands respect. I return to these forests often in my writing and in my imaginings, and each time I'm transformed in some small way by a presence that transcends time and space, reaching beyond cultural boundaries and beyond the generations I can count.

WAVES

Armies of waves knock the coast. Row after row, they roll and crash in thunderous bursts of foam and spray. After each thrust, a fast retreat. Offshore waters gather, converge, renew their commitments, their intentions to lunge towards land. Unlike armies of men or packs of hungry beasts, waves never tire or complain, nor do they die or lie still.

*

Like the pliant branches of willow, leafy appendages that bend and sway at the mercy and whim of wind, jagged sea rocks add voice and momentum to the sea waves. Columns of water engulf the fractured rocks; in their wakes, twisting white corridors waterfall to sea.

Sandpipers scamper at the tide mark. They poke long beaks through sand, hunting for small creatures that thrive where the water slaps the shore.

*

The child digs in the sand until her nails break. She builds castles, forts, schools and churches. Moats surround the towering walls; harbors and dams trap water that whooshes in from the ocean. Such freedom—to build or transform; to shape and mold; to destroy and annihilate towers and tunnels. Waves are enemies. Her task: to build moats and rivers close to the water, yet far enough to withstand the battering waves. The waves strike again and again and again. She outwits their numbers, their sly advance. The work is hard. She moves fast before another wave advances and crushes her outer walls.

Once she made a sea goddess with large mounds of sand for breasts and a tangle of seaweed for pubic hair. She built the sand woman away from the waves; the sculpted form lasted as long as she stood guard.

*

Winds meet the waves head-on, knocking tufts of sea spray off the breakers. Shadows of white foam arch backwards. Against the incoming tides, counter waves of mist.

*

The child discovers a tiny, perfume-sized glass bottle in a junk drawer at home. Every time she forages through the drawer, she finds the bottle. The label reads: "Water from the River Jordan." When she shakes vigorously, the water waves and froths.

At night she dreams of the River Jordan whose magical waters flow through desert mountains. One day she unscrews the black plastic cap and takes a quick swig. The water is clear; there is no taste. Later she worries, "What if the water is poisoned or polluted?" Months later she looks at the bottle and sees slimy orange filaments and black flecks floating at the bottom. Out of clear water, orange and black gunk appears. Gunk that is now in her stomach. When her mother asks what happened to the water in the bottle, she doesn't let on that she knows.

*

Water bashes a path through stone, chisels caves and tunnels in solid rock. Sea cliffs crumble and abandon their outposts at the edge of land. At the shoreline, rocks rubbed and polished by a million tides glisten. The child gathers smooth pebbles, glossy with sea dew. At home the glorious agate, jade, and carnelian sea polish turn charcoal gray.

*

The child remembers the day a service man wheeled a television set into her home. Her father plugged it into a wall in the living room. Every night after that her family sat on the couch and watched places they'd never been to and people they've never met.

The child watches a tidal wave on the weather news. The wave rises higher than a pier and jostles boats in the harbor.

The wave is larger than any she imagines. She starts to have nightmares about tidal waves.

*

At the blowhole, water blasts skyward through the gap in the rock. As the foam sprays overhead, winds shove the geysers back to sea. From a distance, against the dark land where the water spouts high, winds launch small clouds of mists, galloping white stallions and elephants walking on their hind legs.

*

Waves wash over the prickly sea rocks. Succulent kelp curtains the raw surface, softens the harsh outline. As water slides back into the sea, the soaked, rust-colored kelp catches the light, a thousand glints of sun.

*

Hollywood waves flash across the television screen: at the end of a deep valley, a huge concrete and steel-enforced dam holds back an entire lake. The placid water jiggles behind the dam; sluices drain the overflow casually, to relieve pressure. Suddenly a giant crack forks through the cement. In an explosion of concrete and water the dam crumbles.

Movie plots vary: in one a villain blows a dam up with sticks of dynamite. In another, heavy rains drain into the lake. As the water level rises, the ground shakes and rumbles as if an earthquake erupts. The dam isn't designed to hold so much water.

First a crack in the dam wall snakes through the concrete. Then a waterfall tumbles over the side. Soon slabs of concrete toss in the plunging waters which careen down the narrow valley in one huge massive, angry wall. The water rips and crushes houses, busses, people, roads, and trees. The pounding force of tons and tons of water slosh and crash against the mountain walls. Rapid and sure destruction.

*

Between the rocky ridges of the headlands, waters nudge and jostle back and forth in the narrow inlet. Waves surge in triangular peaks before the overriding current knocks them shoreward.

*

Like an old woman furiously shaking her bedspread in the wind, between the tideline and the breaking swells, a cloth-like lacy foam spreads over the blue water. Each passing swell rumples the foamy sea bed.

*

In the movie "The Ten Commandments" God stills the buckling, vibrant waves and opens a corridor in the water, a safe path for Moses to walk across the Red Sea floor. Parallel walls of water tower magically above him. The sea bottom is smooth like a dirt road. Where are the coral reefs, the child wonders, or the wrecked pirate ships or the rocky underwater caverns? Once Moses passes, the towering walls of water cave in, tumble together and cover his pursuers in a crush of violence and destruction.

*

The child sights a black whale offshore. At each swell of ocean, the rock submerges. Where her eyes focus, the form reappears—immense, black and stationary. After the surge passes, the rock veers up, giddy and triumphant, birthing itself into a new world.

*

The mother of the child comes to the sea to mourn. In the contest to outcry, outshout the waves, she loses. However she moans, loud or grief-stricken, the wind and surf muffle her voice.

Infinity is the great truth the sea teaches. Infinity not of life but of forces, powers, and lifelike energies. Waves never cease. After death, waves will go on crashing and retreating, singing and scolding. This comforts the woman.

Minutes and hours no longer count. She rises up off the sand and pulls her parka over her head. She walks back to town, family, home. Like a small treasure she keeps to herself, she carries her loss deep within.

*

The child prepares for the great tidal wave. She listens for the hiss. The tsunami roars like a thundering train in a distant tunnel, the Japanese say. If she's caught offguard at the beach and a huge wave towers overhead, she'll dive straight into the swell before the water has a chance to crash down on her. This is a surfing technique: either ride the crest, or dive into the swell to offset the danger of getting crushed under the weight of a collapsing wave. She'll punch any sharks straight in the nose and kick and scream. Sharks have sensitive noses; their nose is the only place they'll feel a blow.

The child vows never to drown or die.

DECEPTIONS IN GRAY

Scenes from the Northwest

A ferry pulls out from the dock. Pungent oil-slicked pilings creak and sway with the force of the boat relinquishing its grip.

There are times when the sky and water mirror each other, variants of gray separated only by a duller gray outline of a distant coast.

Like a movie in slow motion, the farther the boat travels from the waterfront, the more the port recedes into itself.

The calm expectations of regret, of loss by departure, are underscored by a constant whirring.

*

To stand by the clothesline in the backyard, I must straddle lettuce beds. My feet are coated with damp, loose earth. Beyond the houses across the alley, downtown buildings rise in the southwest, a freeway shimmers, the Olympics define the western horizon.

I pick up a pair of my son's jeans. A shake unwrinkles the pants, still warm from the final rinse. I can barely force a wooden clothespin over the stiff waistband folded across the line.

This landscape is drab, colors mute. Many days pass without sun. Gray is so constant it is reassuring: asphalt, distant factories, the sky with its small miracles of light and progenies of moisture.

My eyes are so accustomed to the half-lights of winter, when clouds gape and a shaft of light breaks, the brightness is harsh. Like a mole I squint; the gray shiny as chrome.

I've come to accept the gray and read it like a text. On a dry day, the height of the clouds, the density of shadow, the pert breezes, I know my wash will dry. If I waited for sun to hang my clothes, they would never dry.

*

A study in gray is an act of reduction. A charcoal sketch reduces a landscape of vivid colors into basic forms and shadows. Autumn leaves, a woman's blush, bowls of sliced apples, oranges and kiwi—to render these in pen and ink or charcoal is to transfer or reduce the patterns, shapes and densities into black and white, with their proliferations of gray.

Likewise distance reduces the precision of details into the vagueness of gray. A mountain seen from a great distance is a blur of gray. Leaves, twigs, earth, foliage, wildlife . . . the totality of nature melds into a uniform color, tinted by light at dusk and dawn, by snow in winter. The Olympics on my horizon loom in and out of focus, a preponderance of grays.

*

In the morning moisture on the glass fogs the outdoors. Overnight a mist materialized, condensed on my window. The gray tarpaper roof next door, the sagging gutter, the sky through the dark firs, these landmarks are duller versions of themselves.

The glass cluttered by countless half-domes of moisture presents a thick transparency. Tiny particles, too small to be called drops, too scattered to be considered water, these beadlike clusters create the vagueness of mist. Yet, when I peer closely, nose to the glass, the uniform arrangement, the individuality of specks is certain.

In summer, looking out a screen door, tiny crisscrossing wires fracture the view. Yet my eyes adjust, compensate. The pinhole squares between the wires, of light, of foliage, when pieced together appear whole. Only the view is hazy.

As I look at the moisture inside the window, I wonder if my eyes see through the half-domes, or through the space between them. Water in a glass is clear, but extracted from air, and scattered on a plane, the effect is filmy and gauze-like.

With opened palm I wipe the tropics from my room, and make a porthole to peer through.

*

Wind from the west clatters rain on my front windows. At night beads gather on the glass, catching the street light with little convex mirrors. Drops, a flickering in each, run, fall, and collide on the outer slopes of the pane.

The force of the wind splatters a raindrop, when it hits the glass, into many smaller drops. But water, once situated on a surface, becomes more congenial, commingling rather than colliding. Like mercury, water gathers into itself, seamless and burgeoning until the mass is too heavy to resist gravity. Runways streak the black night, lined with glitter. One bulbous mass after another tracks the night's weather.

*

What defines rain but the transmutation of cloud into falling particles? The descent is not uniform or symmetrical but heavy and consistent, a dramatic downdrift if only for an instant. Rain is not limited to water and ice: there is the rain of rice after a wedding, the rain of confetti at New Year. Coins, gravel, chicken feed, light in a comet's tail or shooting star, sand, salt, dirt or abusive words—these are all possibilities.

A scattered gathering, airborne and erratic, ultimately succumbs to the invisible force of descent. Rain is a release.

*

On an interior plane, on a shelf or the vast field of a piano top, a steady downdrift perpetuates an inner rain of gray without sound, smell or moisture.

When I sweep, polish or vacuum minute particles gather en masse. It is this congregation of motes, a collective dust and the ubiquitous, slow, gray, anomalous drift that marks the climate of closed spaces.

There is also the gray of interior distancing, the reduction of memory. Hazy gray areas out of recall, out of focus, mark the irretrievable, the dirge of senility, the loss of precision.

As a child I watched sun penetrate windows. Rays and beams, angular and warm, highlighted spots of linoleum or carpet. Without wind, dust in the path of sun sparkled with light. Light transformed the gray of dust, absorbed the dull opaqueness and engendered translucence. Even moon, that deceptive luminescence in black, if denied light and viewed close up, is reduced to a wasteland of perpetual, indelible gray.

*

Some mornings an inner rain patterns my window. Streaks are stalks of marsh grass, erect, linear, and I'm in an aquarium, looking out. Vertical slashes confirm where waters, in their gregarious joinings, trace the shortest route downward. Vaguely parallel bars edge a pathway through a uniform condensation, illuminating strips of an outer world.

Winters are mild by the sound, but one year a pocket of air sandwiched between the glass and frozen outdoors on one side, and the lowered shade on the other side, combined with moisture gathered during the night and created such lush conditions that giant fern fronds sprouted overnight, wild and primeval, frozen in ice.

*

I show my daughter the mist. When we peer out her upstairs window, branches disappear above the trunks in the yard. We cannot see leaves or buds. As if the smaller objects lose identity and meaning. A vaporous density clouds the outside world, softening the edges, a conspiracy of disguise.

But at dusk when the street lights come on, stand under a light, I tell her. Look up into mist. See how the light catches on each small particle, defining it. Look closely; it is never fuzzy.

The sharp precision of globes, minuscule gleamings, is so fine, neither our eyes bared to the sky or an outstretched tongue can feel the gentle downdrift.

UPWIND, DOWNWIND

Leaves

Every weekday morning on my way to work in Seattle, I drive by an urban gardener. He is as punctual as I am. He whooshes the nozzle of his hand-held blower back and forth as I drive by. Where he points his nozzle, the force of the air blasts leaves, dirt and debris neatly away. When the blowing is complete, the sidewalks appear swept, even the street gutters are clean.

In the city there is no need to rake and sweep. With blowers, urban gardeners save time. They easily air-blast leaves off the pavement or lawn and into the gutter. There the wind picks up the leaves and sweeps them away, to deposit them elsewhere down the street. No doubt there is a gardener upwind who first launched his leaves into the breeze where they were carried downwind to settle. If everyone downwind had blowers, the leaves would stay afloat, tumble by without ever settling, and eventually disintegrate in a lengthy airborne journey, joining other airborne particles: dirt, volcanic ash and soot.

Not all gardeners operate the blowers. I picture those that don't scowling upwind as I do, wondering if the inundations of clattering, useless dead leaves each fall is somehow greater now since the leaf blowers started working up the street.

What the Winds Carry

When a volcano erupts, it matters where the winds blow. Upwind from the fiery crater the sky is picturesque: huge billowing clouds rise and puff in intricate tufts of smoke and ash. Fabulous formations of flying dragons, wind goddesses and marauding elephants rise into a turquoise sky. Downwind the rains turn sloggy. A wet mush of ash and soot slops down, clogging roads, driveways, gutters, and radiators.

When Mount St. Helen's in Washington state erupted recently a solemn gray cloud moved east. In Idaho and eastern Washington, miles from the volcano, there were no liquid jewels of transparent and sweet raindrops. Debris-laden winds carried testimonials in ash. The rain turned muddy and ominous. Gray smudge splotched automobiles and clothes; clouds dropped pumice and soggy soot hundreds of miles from the crater. Pellets stung as if fired from a cannon. If residents did not know a volcano had erupted many miles to the west, they might think the sky was falling.

The Advance of the Tumbleweeds

In West Texas winds measuring forty miles per hour are common. Occasional gusts reach ninety-eight miles per hour. When heavy winds stir up dust, a choking, ragged air seeps through closed car windows and drivers experience limited visibility.

One day a driver drove down the freeway from Rankin to Midland. Suddenly a looming obstacle blocked the road. The driver got out of his car and scratched his head. Apparently the wind had swept up hundreds of prickly tumbleweeds and deposited the mass on the highway in the middle of the open prairie.

The tumbleweed is one of the few plants that can grow and survive in the hot, dry Texas plateau. When a tumbleweed reaches maturity, the plant dries and withers. The stem folds in and detaches from the roots so when a strong wind blows the plant is nudged out of place and sent spinning over the dusty land, dispersing seeds with each bounce.

In wide open Texas country, not many barriers inhibit the seasonal excursion of the tumbleweed. Barbed-wire fences are common obstacles. Weeds could blow up against an overpass but overpasses are few and far between on the open stretch of highway. The driver wondered how the tumbleweeds arrived at this spot of highway. Perhaps there wasn't a barrier to impede their journey; maybe the wind suddenly died and they just stopped en masse. Maybe a stranded motorist blocked the progress of tumbling weeds and weed after weed piled up and created the mountainous pile. Did the weeds pelt down from above or sweep over the road in a vortex of twirling chaos? Did they arrive one at a time? Was there a plan or destination?

Transient whirlwinds or dust devils with tornado-like funnels suck at the earth as they twist like spinning tops. Possibly a twirling wind sucked countless tumbleweeds into a voracious vacuum which then moved across the land. When the wind suddenly petered out, the weeds were stranded on the highway, inextricably entwined in a thick mass. Or maybe one dense wall swept across the flat land like an advancing army; en route errant weeds joined ranks and when the wall condensed, the weeds piled into an impenetrable heap.

The tumbleweeds on Texas highway 349 congregated with such density, a twenty-foot-high mass swallowed up cars. Another driver who approached the tangle was tempted to forge ahead. A car could burst through, he thought, if the passage was clear underneath. But how to judge the depth of the mass as it loomed up in the distance, a brown mirage on the pavement? Cars may already have plunged into the midst. Drivers might be stuck and awaiting rescue. More weeds could come slamming into the pile at any moment.

One driver who got out of his pickup to inspect the dense blockade saw the rear bumper of a car gleam slightly from inside the dense thicket. He plunged headlong into the towering weeds on a rescue attempt but was unable to push his way through the prickly mass to the trapped driver's door. He reversed directions to summon help from a pay phone.

"We need help out here. Highway 349."

"What's the problem?"

"Tumbleweeds."

"Sir?"

"Weeds! Cars are stuck inside. I can't get to one driver's door."

"Weeds, did you say?"

"Blocking the highway. We need a rescue team. And vehicles: fork lifts, tow trucks, bulldozers. Bring volunteers. And padded gloves!"

When the residents of the city of Mobridge, South Dakota, woke up one November morning, they discovered that the sun didn't shine. Windows opened to dark tunnels in a mountainous pile of thick, dried weeds. Those that could see out saw only chimneys above the tangle. The weeds were packed so tightly against some houses, the owners couldn't force open their front doors.

The giant weeds, a few the size of Cadillacs, thrived in the lake bed of drought-stricken Lake Oahe. After a hefty west wind snapped the stalks, the weeds freely bounced and tumbled their way to town.

During the invasion residents could not start their car engines since sparks from the cars' exhaust might ignite the brittle weeds. It took city crews days to pull the weeds away from the houses. A tractor crushed the tumbleweeds and packed the debris into enormous piles, like bales of hay. A baler picked up the windrows. Towns have been buried before: by avalanches, mudslides, shifting sands or lava flows. But Mobridge has the distinction of being the only town to be buried in a pile of dried weeds. The crews collected sixty bales, each weighing between one thousand and one thousand two hundred pounds. All totaled, thirty tons of prickly, dehydrated, brittle tumbleweed buried the town.

Some Names For Wind

To some the winds mark seasons like monsoon or a time of day like dusk. A woman I know loves the way a wind can slip through her blouse, and like a lover's kiss set each little hair on edge, little goosebumps of pleasure.

The intense dry heat from the *loong* in Bihar, India, drives men and women crazy if they work outdoors without a turban or shawl. In Europe when the *foehn* blows, it is said the relentless hot air gets under the skin, prickles the brain, speeds up a heart's beating.

The dry, lethal *harmattan* winds that blow from the desert of the Sahara derives from the Arabic word for a forbidden or accursed thing. When the Sahara winds move north the *sirocco*'s dusty current picks up moisture crossing the Mediterranean. Some call the easterly winds sweeping over the same inland sea *levanter.* In Yemen the *shamal* moves north across the Arabian peninsula during December and June.

There's the *chinook* which blows off the ocean in Oregon and Washington. The *pampero* in Argentina blows strong, cold blasts of wind from the southwest across the pampas grass. *Blue northers* herald winter rain clouds in the south.

Early cartographers drew the winds whirling out of the puffy angry cheeks of gods. Some winds command farmers to harvest or take shelter. In Tibet each time the wind rustles one of the thousands of colorful cloth flags, the prayers printed on the flags are believed to be spoken aloud, praising the mountain deities. Prayer flags are hung together like clothes on a clothesline, then strung across courtyards and trees on top of mountain passes.

I name winds and inhale their wafts and odors. I watch how wind ripples bunch grass and nods the harebells. Breezes sweep through the canyon where I live and wave the pine branches, wrest cones from the limbs. Wind ruffles the seedlings barely rising above the earth. Rivers of vapors carry as much water as the Amazon; they rise from the equator and move north in twisting currents to the poles. Winds from every direction. There is no direction the wind will not blow. There will always be wind; there will always be movement. Wind whispers the teachings of impermanence in every rustle and stir of plant and grass, of leaf and hair.

Downwind from Disaster

Those who live near the coast are healthy, lucky to breath every day the fresh ocean winds. Salty sea breezes are pure. I want to believe the air that blows across thousands of miles of open sea is untouched by man-made smog and pollutants.

One day an incident thousands of miles away changed the way I think about wind, the land, my place on the earth. After an accident at a Soviet power plant in the city of Chernobyl massive amounts of radioactive particles were unleashed into the atmosphere. The greatest damage was near the site of the disaster. Still, smaller traces of the pollutants rode the winds east. For the first time since the Hiroshima and Nagasaki nuclear bombs were dropped, deadly winds blew east, across the Pacific. The milch cows of Marin, the artichoke farmers in the Imperial Valley, the groves of oranges and grapefruit, the vineyards and pear orchards of Lake County, the land and people, the animals, the crops, the herons and egrets, the black oaks and laurels, the sugar pines and manzanita trees . . . every living thing on the West Coast shared the same fate; they were the first to receive the deadly clouds, perhaps the strongest radioactive fallout, the acid rains of slow painful death.

Those who live near nuclear energy plants and those who don't can both be exposed to radiation. The earth is ever so small if one person's mistake can threaten the lives of all of us.

There is no upwind, away from disaster. Downwind is everywhere; downwind is deadly. There is no place safe from the threat of a nuclear holocaust.

AFTER THE HURRICANE

On extended visits to Houston I frequently pile my books and papers into a car and drive to a friend's beach house in Galveston for the weekend. The Gulf is an hour's drive to the south.

I walk the beach at Galveston with some consistency. My path leads up and down a stretch of Pirate's Beach north to the state park and south to the horse stables. One year I walk the beach every month, another on alternating months, once after seven months. The first two times I walk this strip of Texas coastline it is the season before the hurricane Alicia strikes.

The hurricane so changes the beachscape, signs of the catastrophe are visible a year later. Windy turbulences buffet the coast with such force, destruction and loss are inevitable.

On my beach walks after the hurricane I chart the extent of the loss and find myself making an inventory as if somehow a detailed study might help me understand the violence and possibly avoid a future danger. The vistas of rubble, the apocalyptic aftermath, the landscapes of disaster and climates of extremes mesmerize me.

I have a sense of how dwellings stood before the hurricane, so I recognize the extent of the material loss. I am familiar with the architectural geography of beachfront property. This sense is not so much a knowledge of what kind of buildings exist but rather a sense of where buildings once stood. Their absence is unmistakable.

In afterthought, trying to reconstruct in my mind a house that vanished, only the obvious details come to mind: a Spanish tile roof, the silhouette at sunrise, lounge chairs on a cedar deck. Unlike decay in cities, haunted houses and derelict ruins earn their woeful, frightening reputations through years of neglect or abuse. A hurricane, on the other hand, instantly changes an occupied, modern beach house with all amenities into a complete and utter ruin.

The loss assimilates into distinct stages. The greatest, to use a superlative to signify an absence or non-existence, is total, absolute loss. For instance, once a house stood on a section of beach; now only a vacant lot remains. Remnants survive: a toaster half-buried in the sand, its cord not even frayed; a circular wrought iron staircase leading to open sky; and a sidewalk that dead ends in the sand between two palms. The remnants only hint at a former structure and contribute in no way to establish with certainty the existence of the now vanished house.

At one building site the support poles for a house stand in equidistant rows; the wooden poles emerge from the white sand like some ancient monument, an earth sculpture in a wasteland. I admire the lean visage. The foundation has integrity; through wind and rain it remains intact. But what good is a lone foundation? Where is the house? Can a foundation be true or good if it no longer supports or upholds anything?

In a list that begins with absence and grows from there, the opposite from assuming a whole and subtracting the lost parts, the second greatest loss after the vanished dwelling is the collapsed dwelling. Ruin is complete in both instances; likewise, the essence of shelter and occupancy is missing in both. The remains of the collapsed dwelling evidence structuring of some sort; only the order, the sense of cohesion and integration is absent. Like a pile of Lincoln Logs, the pieces of a collapsed house suggest a former cohesion. A fallen house invites restructuring. The pieces are present and not missing but the boards are splintered, shattered and irrevocably tangled. No restructuring is possible; the shards are unusable.

A partial structure characterizes a third stage of loss: an edifice remains, yet parts are missing. Some houses lack decks, chimneys or walls. The roof and front wall of one house are torn away. I wonder, Did the roof blow off in one piece and land whole somewhere? Or did the roof fall apart shingle by shingle, Spanish tile by Spanish tile?

A house without a front wall invites voyeurs. I peer into the interior. Green drapes billow by a window; the carpeting is beige; the sofa matches the carpet. The owner's life style is evident in the color and floor plan of the kitchen, the pattern of false brick paneling around the fireplace. I feel embarrassingly intimate with people I never met.

Besides the fallen and stricken buildings, there are a myriad of scattered pieces to mentally sort through. Lone objects and haphazard piles of debris signal the devastation months after the catastrophic hurricane sweeps through the neighborhood.

Earthquakes also cause structures to collapse but with a noted difference. Earthquakes are accompanied by dust: dust dislodged from ancient buildings; dust released by the impact of buildings that fall to the ground; dust freed from plaster walls. Beach rubble is not dusty. Maybe the wind disperses dust at the time of the loss of cohesion, the collapse. Maybe plaster is an anomaly in beach house construction. Sand is present but sand, unlike dirt, has distinct form and weight. Sand does not readily take flight. Even if a heavy wind stirs up the sand, the resulting sandstorm is not powdery or dusty. Sand particles manifest a cleanliness.

Beach rubble has a distinct character, unlike the rubble of demolished buildings. Demolition sites in Houston are barren, that is, the rubble consists of building materials: wooden slats, plaster, shards, pipes and broken glass. Before the demolition, salvage workers remove doors, frames, knobs and fixtures; auctioneers cart away the furnishings. The rubble of a collapsed beach house, on the other hand, includes domestic articles: rugs, utensils, draperies, bicycles. The resulting heap is consequently large, fuller, ripe with context.

In one pile of debris a refrigerator juts out halfway from the heap. Refrigerators do not collapse. In the rubble, a refrigerator still occupies a large, rectangular space. Even a refrigerator blown from a vanished house probably lands somewhere intact—a garage, perhaps, the bottom of a bayou, or a shopping mall parking lot. Suddenly I place great faith in the indestructibility of refrigerators. If a refrigerator takes flight, what amount of tumbling over sand, over pavement will it take to dislodge a door, break up the metal body? Surely there must be refrigerators out there that appear after a hurricane more or less intact—maybe a door is missing, a side dented or a corner crushed.

I resolve to write my name and address inside my refrigerator after I drive home. I won't write it on the door; doors fall off, the hinges are not indestructible. Below my name I'll offer a reward to the finder. Like a note in a bottle set to sea or the message attached to a helium-filled balloon, in the advent of a hurricane I'll be able to chart the progress of a dislodged and errant appliance.

I circle a mound of one collapsed dwelling. The mound is not symmetrical but the center towers above the rest of the debris. Unlike the pile of leaves in my backyard where a slow, inevitable deterioration induced by mold sets in every fall, one year after the hurricane Alicia, there is no rot or decay. No mold grows at the beach. Does the salt air and sand inhibit this process? There is no rust, either. The chrome dinette chair leg that sticks out of the mound still gleams.

It occurs to me that a vocabulary of ruin is sketchy, as is a vocabulary of chaos. We define objects by the order we place on them, or by their relationship to an order that surrounds them. A chair, for instance, has four legs, a seat, and a back. But how to describe a part of a chair precisely? A portion of a chair ripped apart by a hurricane? It is cumbersome to dissect the parts and name individually which parts remain: e.g., the front leg on the righthand side as I face the chair is attached to one third of the seat, broken at odd angles with the ladder back in disarray since the third rung is missing, the fourth splintered, etc.

Another thing: domestic artifacts make haunting beach debris. Since beaches are pristine by definition, any item that washes ashore, cast by water or wind, is considered debris. A ridiculous scene: a couch at high tide. Impossibly cumbersome, a couch could not have washed ashore. There are likewise no telltale signs of a prolonged ocean float, no barnacles, no seaweed bits. A couch at high tide is incongruous. A mattress, on the other hand, is more mobile. Who hasn't seen abandoned mattresses under freeways, in the woods? But a beached davenport, a drift sofa? Impossible. A sea gull pecks stuffing from the arm-rest like a vulture pecks at a corpse.

I consider a floral printed bedsheet. Only an elastic corner of the carnation-and-lily designer sheet pokes out from between two nondescript masses of debris. The bedsheet appears fresh, crisp, even though the cloth wrinkles and bunches. Like the cottons I hang out to bleach naturally in the sun, perhaps this sheet's spanking white background benefits from the prolonged exposure. How else to explain the lack of deterioration?

Another fragment invites speculation: a lone light bulb, no, two unscathed light bulbs couched in pockets of sand. Over the year wind drove sand particles up and around the fragile glass spheres to create globe-shaped pockets of sand. The encroaching sand now cushions the bulbs. Unharmed, ironic in their persistence, their fragility, the bulbs proclaim their testimonies. No sand particles scratch the glass; the bulbs appear new. I'm tempted to take one home and screw it into a socket. If the light works, I can prove to myself some further irony: while the entire house including the socket in which the bulb is screwed collapsed and disintegrated, this delicate object of light, warmth and domesticity remains unscathed.

When I focus on the ironies of mishap, the odd bits of rubble, the dislocations and chaos, I think, What if I'm caught in a hurricane? A wave of vulnerability and fear sweeps over me. If wind uproots my body, tosses and slams me against the ground, I will not survive. To confront a hurricane is sure death.

Do not worry, I assure myself. To maintain a constant fear of death is futile. The moment of death, while unpredictable as to time and place, is nevertheless inevitable. Death might come at any time. Death may even be quicker than a Texas hurricane that upheaves and howls for hours on end.

In the chaos of shock following disintegration, in the footsteps of disaster, I pick at the pieces and try to make sense of the randomness. If I count miracles like the unharmed light bulbs, the harm diminishes. That is, disaster is not complete or total if fragile light bulbs survive. To witness disorder in isolated heaps of ruin on an otherwise pristine beach is a lesson in fate and the laws of impermanence. Ultimately the external ephemera, the disorder, is outside of myself; this is both a sobering vision and a profound relief.

TWO MEN FROM THE SEA

In the film two men carry a large wardrobe out of the sea. The wardrobe is too cumbersome for one to carry alone; two men are needed. Never mind how they emerge, smiling, between crashing waves on a beach with this piece of furniture in their arms. On shore they shake water out of their ears and admire themselves in the mirror on the wardrobe door. The wood is not waterlogged and their berets, though soaked, did not shrink.

The men never open the drawers nor the door behind the mirror, and it seems no belongings or necessities are stored there. The men only carry the wardrobe, always in agreement as to where to go, though sometimes they stop to make decisions. There is time for somersaults and flirting with a girl, but when they try to crowd into a tram and into a crowded restaurant carrying, of course, the wardrobe, they are unsuccessful and arouse hostile reactions from the people in those places.

City thugs beat the men up. One is thrown against the mirror, breaking it. The other revives him with water hoisted up from a pier in his upturned beret; as he pulls, most of the water splashes out of the hat that is suspended on a long rope. The men do not abandon the wardrobe even though they are exhausted, and a hotel manager refuses them lodging because of it.

They reach a beach. Maybe it is the same beach they emerged from, maybe it isn't. Without landmarks like trees or houses, all beaches look alike.

They carry the wardrobe across the beach and out into the sea. Their bodies shrink as they move farther out and soon the two men disappear in the water. Waves do not hinder them and nothing washes ashore.

THE BIG QUAKE

In the fifties I was a student at the old Mayfield Elementary School, a historic, now demolished, structure in Palo Alto, located just five miles from the San Andreas fault. Every six months the principal, Mr. Papagni, walked the empty corridors during class and cranked an old-fashioned siren. This announced a surprise earthquake drill. At the sound of the first wailing, we crouched under our desks. The second siren signaled the all-clear.

Mrs. Dowell, the teacher, taught us to squat under a sturdy table at home or stand in the portal of a doorway during an earthquake. That way if the roof fell in we would be protected. One time I kneeled on a thumbtack trying to crouch under my desk. She drew a rough map on the blackboard: California in white chalk and the San Andreas fault a solid blue line running through our town. "The earthquakes are caused by shifting plates," she explained. "When the plates rub against each other, the ground shakes."

I had my own theories. A subterranean creature lived in the earth and seasonally turned over, I thought, causing the earth above to move slightly. Or, in a den beneath our town an enormous grizzly slept away the winters. Grizzly dens were cramped so occasionally the bear needed to stretch out a limb, or suddenly flex a muscle. When the grizzly moved, the earth was set in motion. Once when my stomach growled with hunger, I thought that could be an explanation, too. Maybe the huge denizen of the deep was hungry and the gyrations of land were caused by the growling of an empty, primordial stomach.

Gentle earthquakes did rock up through the wooden floors and jiggle the desks at school or my bed in the upstairs bedroom with an eerie regularity. I daydreamed about the big quake, the one that was predicted—at worst—to sever the state of California or part of it, from the continental United States. What if the big quake hit during the sock hop or when I was knocking on doors trying to sell Girl Scout cookies? If the quake hit when I was swimming at the club, could I feel the vibrations in the water? Would the waves slosh over the side of the pool? What if I was locked in the soundproof listening booth at the record store with Little Richard on full blast, could I tell a heavy bass beat from a ground tremor?

Earthquakes became a natural expectation. I sharpened my sense of touch. My whole body could sense if a building swayed from the ground up, or moved from some other cause, like a heavy person climbing the stairs. A passing garbage truck or a jack-hammer at work on the pavement set off other distinct vibrations.

If I couldn't pinpoint a tremor, I checked for earthquake signs: chandeliers swinging overhead, blue willow dishes rattling out of the cupboards, the green Mexican handblown glasses crashing on the marbled linoleum. Like other forms of wild weather, earthquakes were unpredictable and dangerous: I needed to be prepared. I couldn't control the violent natural elements outside my home, but I could plan ways to cope.

I studied movies and photos from the great San Francisco quake of 1906. When the earth did open up, the split was never wider than a ten- or twelve-foot chasm, I figured. And these chasms were not necessarily deep. If one opened up on the road, a car would fall ten feet, at most. An inconvenience, but not a life-threatening situation.

Or, say I was stranded in the field behind the school and the earth opened up. A ten-foot crack would break slowly, and give me time to jump out of the way. My dictionary defined chasm as a "yawning fissure." Surely a yawning fissure was one which opened up slowly or lazily, like a yawning mouth.

To envision the worst, if I did fall into a burgeoning crack, I would not die. I might even scramble up again unscathed. If I was outdoors when the big quake hit, I knew I could survive. Even if I was indoors, since I could detect the earthquake vibrations, I was confident I could vacate any building I was in. The trick was to vacate before the building collapsed.

San Francisco had many skyscrapers. When a ten-story building tumbled, I figured, ten floors of belongings would pile on top of each other. If a building had an average of five apartments per floor, that totaled fifty apartments, or the personal belongings of up to a hundred people that could be jumbled in the mass of ruin.

I figured I could survive a quake, but what about the house? If our two-story house collapsed, my family's belongings: clothes, mementos, furniture, food and knickknacks would tumble into a heap of tattered rubble, an instant pile of debris.

The earthquake photos had one element in common: complete chaos. At night in bed, I prayed the quake would not hit when I was asleep.

From time to time, especially on a rainy day, I wandered about the house poking into closets and drawers, as if this search might be useful someday, to restore a lost order. Or maybe this snooping gave me a sense of what to expect in terms of the impending disorder. I was fascinated by the medicine cabinet in the bathroom. Aspirin bottles and cough syrup remedies shared a shelf with goldfish flakes from a time my brother had goldfish. Mosquito repellent and flashlight batteries bubbling with rust were crammed next to brushes from the Fuller Brush man and samples from the Avon lady.

Here was natural disarray. I puzzled over the mix, certain a secret order existed, only I didn't know what it was. A bottle of glue nudged a chartreuse Mexican donkey ceramic; the pack on the donkey's back held mismatching glazed copper cuff links I had made in art class. Ashtrays sported matches even though no one in my family smoked. The matchbooks featured faraway restaurants, advertisements for body-building magazines, breast cream developers or special collector's stamps to send away for for only $1.00.

Although the medicine cabinet housed bottles of medicines, they were crusty around the cap, and had bypassed their potency expiration dates. Bottles remained in the cabinet for years: crusty milk of magnesia or kaopectate, reminders of sicknesses my family had overcome. Castor oil, thick, brown and ominous, was a cure-all my mother favored long before I was old enough to read the faded, stained label. The cabinet was a gathering place for strange pills, potions and bottles that were no longer useful, but worth hanging onto just in case an emergency arose.

Even more curious were the junk drawers in the kitchen, dining and living rooms, out-of-the-way drawers at the end of a table or in the pantry, catchalls for innumerable odd bits. Lost and one-of-a-kind items ended up in the junk drawer. I'd poke through dust and pointed edges of stray needles, pocket knives and tacks, looking for treasures. Coins, marbles or buttons always appeared at the bottom of a junk drawer.

I was attracted to the jumble, the chaos, as if the drawers were a microcosm of the larger world, the collapsed buildings, the jumbled heaps of belongings after an earthquake. The more I poked into the drawers, the more the disorder became predictable. I had a sense of what was where, what junk was in which junk drawer. The disarray was confined to a particular space.

True junk, according to Webster's, is worthless trash. I disagree. A potential use differentiates junk in a drawer from trash. Most important, each cluster, though chaotic, was undeniably mysterious. Some days I'd open a drawer and gaze at the contents. Inside I'd study the chaos that could easily symbolize the demise of order, the apocalyptic aftermath of an unfortunate deviation in weather, a weird inundation from above or below ground. But in the disorder, ultimately I saw a lost order, a potential order. When I gazed into a junk drawer I'd lose myself in a reverie where future hypothetical needs were jumbled with past encounters and discards.

Still there was the dilemma of how to prepare for the impending earthquake. If my belongings could be ordered in such a way as to survive intact if our home collapsed, it would be much easier to retrieve my possessions. One day I rescued a shoe box from the incinerator. The vacant, four-sided box was a handy storage chamber. Immediately dozens of possibilities emerged. Some uses I thought of: to store similar things like rocks or coins (lucky pennies and Indian head nickels) or jewelry like pop-bead necklaces, charm bracelets and turquoise seashell strands; to hide valentines, love notes or Halloween candy. Most important, in the event of an earthquake, a box automatically preserved the contents. A box could easily be retrieved from under a pile of debris. Boxes provided a solution; if I stored everything neatly in boxes, my possessions could survive the earthquake.

Soon my closet was filled with boxes. Postage stamps filled an odorous cigar box. First-Day-of-Issue envelopes lined the bottom, forever scented with the pungent aroma of tobacco and cedar. The box protected my rare collection of stamps from countries I couldn't find on a map, like San Marino and Togoland. The tinier the country, it seemed, the more colorful and unusual the stamps were, as if bold triangles or shocking pinks compensated for obscure geography.

My jewelry box had a Cinderella figurine that twirled to music every time I opened the lid the slightest crack. A transparent yellow slide-rule lid slipped in and out of a red plastic pencil box. I stacked white Easter gloves, the fingers always half the length of mine, in one of father's flat necktie boxes. I filled my sewing basket box with thimbles, scissors, threads, and notions. On my dresser a ceramic box with a rose on the lid held barrettes, bobbie pins and rubber bands. One of mother's flat nylon stocking boxes was perfect for hankies I pressed, folded and tucked away, ready to use, but afraid to soil. Mother stored woolens through the summer in the cedar chest, a huge boxlike compartment at the foot of her bed.

I arranged shells on beds of cotton bandaging, in large, heavy, white Emporium gift boxes I saved from Christmas. Paper dolls were stored in one of mother's hat boxes; I cut the Betsy McCall series out from *Jack and Jill* magazine. Every month I'd hunt and clip the paper doll page. The wardrobe changed each season: sun suits in August, snow jackets and ice-skating costumes in December.

On rainy days or during nap times, I'd open up a box and sort through the items. My collections prepared me for a future time when I might need to make a trade, or locate materials for a school project like the science fair where I could show off my agates and petrified wood. There was also an element of admiration. Some days I just opened a box and gazed at the contents, proud of owning such orderly and unique items.

A collection was a connection to some greater order and identity. I could tame the peril, outsmart the destruction from an impending quake, I figured, if I ordered and stored everything I owned in boxes. As long as I had my collections neatly sheltered in cardboard, wooden, or ceramic boxes, I was prepared for the big quake.

DREAMING AND DRIVING

Except for a seven year period when I lived abroad and the two years I attended graduate school in Texas, I've been driving my whole adult life. Driving is, in fact, a frequent activity. I enjoy driving, manipulating a vehicle; I acknowledge the convenience of having a car to drive when and where I want to go regardless of the weather and I recognize the daily necessity of driving a car to get to the store, the library, the office, the coffee shop and home again. In fact driving is so automatic I can—as the old adage goes—drive in my sleep and often do.

Since childhood I've had driving dreams. The first were nightmares. Sometimes the car headed up a road so steep I'd fear the car would slip backwards and fall. Once the car edged up a drawbridge as the bridge raised to a perpendicular angle. A recurring dream combines strange landscapes and weird weather conditions. The car travels on a perilous roadway surrounded on both sides by water. The wind is wild; waves lunge toward the car, splashing on the road which turns into a narrow isthmus bordered by pounding surf. The car proceeds but the road disappears underwater leaving the car stranded.

Cars aren't the only dream vehicles of transport: tractors, aerial balloons, busses, trains, and bicycles frequently appear to carry me somewhere. Even though I may occupy the driver's seat, the vehicle, usually a car or van (my unconscious? my fears? my karma?), often drives me. I may think I'm in control but any confidence is often undermined by the unexpected.

Driving dreams share the momentum of travel: I'm en route somewhere for some reason but there is never any certainty that where I'm going will remain a constant or that I'll ever arrive. Often I'll be headed one place and it turns into another place, another city, another time. Or if I do arrive at the planned destination, it is unrecognizable and resembles a totally different landscape. In one dream I journeyed to Tibet, now a province of California, fifty miles north of Lake Tahoe.

The eerie landscapes of dreams haunt my waking life: avalanching mountain paths, inhospitable climates, an eroding isthmus inundated by crashing waves. Often landscapes turn menacing and danger lurks around every corner. Many dreams are dreams of motion: I'm riding in a car or sitting behind the steering wheel driving as landscapes whoosh by. Rarely are the driving dreams peaceful or passive. At best dream driving offers an escape from dangerous terrain; at worst I'm the driver of an out-of-control car headed straight for disaster.

*

I know the way to the university. The shortcut leads up a cobblestone driveway. A man pulls open a weathered wooden gate as I approach driving the tan Buick. The sedan barely squeezes through the gate. Inside there are crowds of people and I bring the car to a halt in the middle of a Catholic mass. People are on their knees in the aisle. With all these worshippers the aisle isn't large enough for the Buick to crowd through. Luckily the people are friendly; they don't snicker at my car in church.

*

I'm driving a van. An oncoming car approaches in the middle of a two-way turning lane. I'm driving too fast, but quickly slow down and swerve right to avoid the car. Suddenly my eyes shut tight. The driving is not scary but not being able to see where I'm going is. I feel like I'm just waiting for something to hit me. Lori, my assistant, is in the seat next to me. "Lori, can you help me steer?" She puts a hand on the wheel, then answers, "I can't help." I try very hard to open my eyes but they are clenched shut.

*

A husband of mine hustles me out of the house because he is going to set fire to it to collect on the insurance. He puts me in an old wooden milk wagon pulled by a cow. The cow plunges into a big river and paddles towards shore. "Hey," I think. "I don't want the house torched." In an instant, I return home. A stranger is in the house; there is no fire. Then I'm back in the cart pulled by a cow. We plunge again into the river and I think, "How will I ever make it ashore?" The river rounds a big ninety degree bend and the city on the far shore looks promising.

*

An elderly woman from my senior book-discussion group drives me down the road to Paris in a Volkswagen bus. We enter many tunnels that are covered in vines. They remind me of covered bridges except they appear more decorative with luscious grapes and wild blooms. We pass a group of peace protestors and strange black monuments. The road turns mushy. "I'll have to turn around," she says. "The road isn't any good." Before she can turn, the van dips into an enormous mud puddle and halts abruptly. The front third of the bus is immediately submerged. I pick up my briefcase but it's too late. The soupy mud has reached my knees and my briefcase full of important papers is all muddy.

*

I'm on a high cliff, overlooking an island. Huge pelicans fish in the distance. They soar down to the water, and catch fish with their giant beaks. One grabs for an orange I hold out in the palm of my hand. My son and I prepare to ride. We harness a huge basket to a pterodactyl. Its enormous body is perfect for sky sailing. We cast off. The aerial views below are spectacular . . . geometric farmers' fields, a snaking river, a ribbon of highway.

*

I'm six and my parents leave me alone in a parked car. Suddenly the car starts to roll down a steep hill. I scoot over to the driver's seat to steer. I maneuver the car away from oncoming cars and steer free of parked cars but the car won't stop. I stretch my foot but it's too short to reach the brake pedal. The car picks up speed careening downhill. Instantly I drop to the floor and bring the wayward vehicle to a halt by pushing my hand firmly on the brake pedal.

*

A friend is driving up a very steep, mountain road. The upgrade is at least seventy degrees with lots of narrow curves. At every turn I hold my breath. The outside lane is eroding and almost slips off the mountain. Up ahead the lane is crudely attached to the mountain. I can see rusty hinges and long bamboo support poles that extend down the mountain for miles. The poles are crooked and weak. "Watch out for this side of the road," I warn. The road is only tacked on.

*

I drive a tractor and park in town, then I shop for pomegranates in a store. A poet gives me a ride. She drives to the Montauk highway. Then I remember the tractor. "Let me out. I forgot the tractor!" I get out with my bags and hitchhike back to town to pick up the tractor which I drive to the beach. The Atlantic Ocean spreads out like royal blue jello. I set a backpack full of manuscripts down on the sand. The backpack floats out to sea. I grab for it and set the pack back down. The next wave washes it out to sea again.

*

I'm driving the van and make a left hand turn. Suddenly I'm in the walkway of the Pike Place Public Market in Seattle. In front of me are stalls of tomatoes, turnips and apples. The passage is narrow, only five feet wide. The van will never squeeze through the stalls. I can't reverse. How did I get here? Where is the way out?

*

A long hippy bus is parked on the road. I knock on the back door and enter thinking someone I know is inside. The bus starts to move as I walk down the aisle. I exit at a large meadow on a bluff. I'm in a hippy commune, a complete city with stores, library, and people all over, mostly women in long, hoop skirts. I glance at the ocean and the silhouette of two churches on a distant shore. I think: I'd like to stay here longer. Someone gets me the address. I sit on a picnic table. Two hippy men bow down on the ground in some ritual. Up in the sky, flying busses!

*

I drive by an island. A huge hollowed-out tree trunk is suspended thirty feet in the air. I bend down from my driver's seat to peer up at the tree. Then I pass caves, shaped like two foot-wide burrows in the ground. In the morning I notice a piece of a fir tree on top of the covers on the bed. How did it get in my room?

*

I'm staying at a hotel in Mexico. From my room by the river, I watch three friendly seals swim by. The view makes my window seem like an aquarium. I see seals somersaulting under water; then they surface and poke their noses in my direction.

Outside in the market I can't find my car. Where did I park it? It's late and I need to meet my lover. I wander down alleys filled with shops. Serapes, shawls, baskets, and huge pottery vases fill every available space in the alley. Crowds push and shove. I'll never find where I left the car.

*

I'm with a friend running errands on our bikes but I need to unload the van. Before I do, I slip into a restroom at a college. The tiled floor is at an eighty-degree angle to the wall. I stagger to the toilet stall and sit on the tilted seat. Because of the tilt shit drops on my white dress. I brush it off, but the shit smears all over. Then shit is in my mouth—like peanut butter, sticky, yucky, awful. Gasp! To wash up I stick my finger into my mouth to dislodge the shit. Soon the drain is plugged with shit. Then the water from the tap is laced with shit. Shit is everywhere.

*

I'm in an auditorium waiting for a reading to begin. I leave my purse on a seat and go out into the lobby. When I return a lady is in my seat. "That seat is saved," I tell her. I try to be polite. She doesn't answer me. I go upstairs to look for another seat. The manager tells me I'm on in ten minutes. "Oh! I'm the reader! But I don't have my book with me," I tell him. "Get one," he says.

He's right. How can I read without my book? I don't have my work memorized. I remember I'm at the World's Fair and my book is available across the grounds at the bookfair. A friend offers to drive her red Dodge to speed things up. I get in. We sail past clowns and jugglers. We near a steep embankment. "Do I go up here?" she asks the way. "Yes, the bookfair is over there," I point. However, before I can tell her she is not on a road, the car slides down an embankment and overturns. I gasp as the car rolls over. We are O.K. but the car, the tires especially, are totally demolished. Luckily I have insurance. I need to fill out an accident report. A guard opens his wallet and gives me a form. It is four pages long and the writing is tiny. Wait! I can't fill this out now. I have only five minutes before my performance! I climb steps leading up to a fortress. The huge gate is locked. I need to pass the elephant cage next to the display tent, but where is it?

*

I drive the Buick in my hometown neighborhood which is an hour's drive from Santa Cruz, the nearest beach. Castelleja Street is now one-way. As I turn onto the street it begins to climb and turns into a steep, new overpass. The road rises from where the railroad tracks are, and arcs over the high school, over the fields and roads. When the street finally arcs back down I drive off onto a cliff overlooking the beach. "A super expressway," I think, "straight to the Pacific."

I don't recognize the beach. The road is rocky and steep. Thundering waves crash up and cover the road. The road begins to crumble in places. I'm afraid the road will wash into the sea. I reverse and I drive back to the beach. As the car straddles the waves, half in and half out of the water, I think: it's wet here but safer than the road.

*

I get my period and stay home in bed. A friend visits and suggests I could sell used tampons to researchers looking for medical data. "They want used tampons?" I ask incredulously. She nods. I could use the money . . . "Come on," my lover says, "Let's go." He takes my bike and books while I walk across a bridge. On the other side the road is rocky and slippery. I leave my pack with my wallet and camera at the bottom of a hill. After a ten minute jeep ride I end up alone in a kayak in the river. I pass beautiful black falls. Rapids loom up ahead so I paddle towards shore. I pull the kayak ashore and step out onto an old carved sandstone temple. A piece breaks off and crashes into the water. A baby leopard and a koala bear sit in a tree. I stare at the creatures to make sure they don't attack me from behind. Where is my pack?

*

I'm riding in a jeep and holding up a flag. There are three others in the jeep. I wear a red t-shirt. People in a foreign country line up along the road. I'm the leader of the demonstration which is in favor of revolution. This is risky, I think. Red signifies the revolution and I'm wearing a red t-shirt. What if I'm arrested? To fool the police, I'll take off the red t-shirt and throw it to the crowd.

*

Jack Nicholson calls. "Want to go to the movies?" he asks. "Sure," I say. I greet him downstairs in my bathrobe. "Wait a second," I apologize. "I'm not dressed yet." I put on make-up, pants and shoes, then change to a dress before changing back into pants. I look around for my glasses and purse. Dressing takes forever. I hope he waits. He does. When he opens the car door for me I notice two elderly ladies sitting in the back seat of his car. "Good," I think. "he brought escorts." He drives along a coastal road. I look down at the waves crashing far below. At each screeching turn my heart flutters in my throat. "How about 'Joan of Arc'? he asks. "O.K. with me."

*

Not all dreams manifest at night. During the day I often find myself daydreaming inside a moving vehicle. The act of driving is conducive to dreaming. The monotony of the predictable pattern of white slashes in the road, the consistency of a flattened, bumpless roadway or the slowly changing terrain of a massive traffic jam are ripe conditions for dreaming. Watching these repetitious scenes reminds me of the proverbial remedy for falling asleep—counting identical sheep which lumber up from the imagination to leap a fence, rhythmically, one by one.

Daydreaming is a fertile escape from the tedium of mechanicality. I'm wary of the irresistible lure that pulls—like Circe luring ancient mariners to a treacherous shore—a daydreamer into a lulling, hazardous sleep. Even with caution dangers abound.

*

When I was five I rode in the back seat of the family car. In a daydream I opened the door a crack and watched the scenery, houses and stores, whoosh by through the slit of metal. The landmarks: red, white and blue was the gas station; green after that was Mrs. Grady's hedge. Somehow the landscape was special when viewed through this wee crack. Once mother was driving and hit a bump. Before I could cry or shout I fell out of the car and landed hard on the pavement. "Mother," I prayed, "Pleeese come back!" I'll never forget the image of the car disappearing down the busy street abandoning me on the pavement. My ankle broke in the fall. I wore a cast for six months.

*

Whenever I drive my car onto the Seattle ferry bound for the Olympic peninsula, I'm cautious of my position on the boat. If my car is the first to board, the crew waves me to the front. "Closer, closer," their hands signal as I slowly inch the car up to the edge of the boat. Finally, "Stop!" I shut off the motor and set the emergency brake extra tight. Only a chain stretches between my car and the restless waters of Puget Sound. I imagine the worst: I'll return from the upstairs lounge at the end of the crossing and find my car vanished overboard.

*

I'm not sleeping but driving to work when I feel a huge noise. I don't hear it with my ears. The sensation is like the sonic booms I heard as a kid growing up near Moffitt Field, California. The sonic booms cracked, then traveled the length of sky from horizon to horizon like thunder. This boom was a tremendous energy combustion, an explosive force that suddenly broke loose, yet it was confined to a moment, a point in time and space.

Two weeks later my father was killed in a head-on crash. His car veered over the dotted line in a mountainous rural road and crashed into an oncoming car. The couple in the other car were unhurt.

I remembered the boom a month after the funeral. Driving over the expansive freeway bridge hundreds of feet over Lake Union in Seattle, with a wave of goosebumps, I felt the boom again. Was the boom a premonition of the head-on crash? Can an abstract sensation be a premonition? That is, not an image of a crash, but of an anonymous, soundless boom like I felt but didn't hear? If so, if I recognized the premonition, could I have prevented the crash? Is a prediction of danger enough to prevent danger? Or only enough to issue a warning, "Be careful"?

*

I'd like to think that when I drive in dreams it is a sign of taking charge of my life, a steadfast determination to make a "go" of things and to steer my way out of adverse situations. I should have some reassurance too, since I've never crashed in my dreams, nor in my day-to-day journeys.

At the corner Stop & Go market I frequently drop a quarter in the slot and take a seat in the Turbo video game car. I grab the steering wheel and press on the accelerator as an incredibly vibrant roadway veers towards me on the monitor. Comic book trees all the same dimensions line the road, followed by street lights set equidistant from each other, a familiar repetitive landscape. As I shift into high, the road speeds faster. Cars leap out of blind corners, approach me in the same lane or crash into me from behind. I wheel in and out of lanes to avoid ambulances, fire trucks, I round sharp curves that drop off into the ocean. Déjà vu. My car leaps over holes, water puddles, and maneuvers on icy, slick roads. When I pass cars, I score points. I am in control, speeding along, practicing for those eerie day and night visions.

IF THE PLANE GOES DOWN

Every time I fly, as soon as the plane taxis down the runway, a stewardess with well-manicured nails pulls an oxygen mask over her hair-do without shifting a single hair out of place. Then she exaggerates inhaling into the mask; I know the procedure by heart.

To be prepared for potential emergencies, I read the emergency instruction pamphlet tucked into the upholstered pouch in front of me. The stiff pamphlet is designed to last for many curious passengers, though most passengers skip reading the instructions. Perhaps they have at one time or another, and have already familiarized themselves with the general content.

If unimaginable weird weather or an unforeseen mechanical problem arises, and the plane is forced to make an unannounced landing, I want to be prepared. If I can remember what to do in an emergency, my chances of survival are good. However, when I study the safety pamphlet more questions than solutions arise.

To begin: A lady who wears a turquoise skirt and matching vest masters her seat belt operation in illustration one. She sits, strapped-in, knees together, the epitome of prim. Next to her, free-floating hands, cut off above the cuff, illustrate how a single finger can lift the seat-belt lock and free the lady.

In all probability, the pamphlet begins with this clearly recognizable and nonthreatening situation so as to build a reader's confidence and stimulate the desire to read on. In reality, the seat belt section is a waste of time. When in distress or doubt, it is far easier to ask a stewardess or a fellow passenger (e.g., "Help me open this, will you?" Or, "How do I undo this blasted thing?" A loud and clear "HELP ME OUT!!" should also bring results).

I browse on. Two symbols are repeated throughout the pamphlet, and if readers understand the bold red arrow to mean follow the direction it is pointing, and a bold red "X" over an object to signify a firm "NO!", then the instructions will also be clear. Lack of language should not impede anyone of any nationality or literacy level from looking at the pictures and understanding the unwritten messages.

As I scan the sequential pictures, I can't help but notice omissions or small inconsistencies. To amuse myself I tally the mistakes as if I were challenged by one of those cartoon puzzles where the reader compares two similar drawings to find which items have been left out of one: a jug with two handles in one picture, for example, has only one handle in the next.

I feel rewarded in some small way when I can point the inconsistencies out. The man who offers his hand to those sliding down a wing tip is an example. He has a mustache in two sequences but not in the third. Beards and mustaches in general, seem to fade in and out of the pictures. The man has also extinguished the lit cigarette, I notice, which dangles from his mouth in an earlier box. The lit cigarette which has a red "X" over it as he walks down the crowded aisle is nowhere to be found in the wing-tip scene.

There follows a series with a mother and son. The mother pulls on her oxygen mask in a record six seconds (a little cartoon clock tells me how long) before pulling on the son's mask. Next a box in the upper corner features one plane diving towards water, and one diving towards a mountain with trees. The passengers are shown with their faces between knees, or heads far forward, their bodies still strapped into their seats. I assume this is the "Brace for Emergency Landing" section. Readers are spared an actual crash, though perhaps an element of optimism is justified. Not all landings are crashes.

To go on, there are three types of emergency exits (provided the plane lands intact). Arrows point to the types of proper exiting procedures. Two of the exits have large yellow self-inflating slides, which operate at the pull of a string (a pull in the direction of the red arrow). The way to descend on the slide is to take a flying leap, bounce somewhere mid-slide, and then glide on down.

Inappropriate descents are also illustrated behind the now familiar large red "X". The lady who sits first, for example, and then shoves off hampers the swift, emergency pace. (Her high heels, by the way, warrant a separate, magnified box with the now customary negative red symbol.) Passengers seated near window exits over the wings can simply slide down the wing tip to safety. (In this case, passengers are not encouraged to take a flying leap.)

Different airlines have slightly different instructions, but they share similar cartoon features. I always pause at the picture of a man who grips a briefcase on which a large red "X" is superimposed. He is featured once at the top of the slide, ready to leap, and also in the act of climbing out a window, only his sweater has changed to a green color for the window picture.

I imagine the concern of the safety officials—if everyone brought a briefcase, someone might drop one and impede exit progress. Or, perhaps it is essential to use both hands on the inflatable slide and if one hand grips a briefcase, the risk of falling off the slide is too great.

Yet I balk when the contents of my own briefcase come to mind: manuscript papers, notes and documents safely tucked under my seat (the cushion of which can convert to a floating block of foam). I cannot comply with the suggestion to abandon my briefcase. Besides enduring the inconvenience of a thwarted plane trip, I'm supposed to part with my life's work at the top of the slide to safety? No way! And anyway, I can negotiate a slide with one hand, no problem. These illustrations are only suggestions, I remind myself. There is no rule or law governing emergency exiting procedures. Certainly clinging to my briefcase is an allowable exception. Better yet, I'll pack a lightweight backpack into the briefcase before I board a plane. That way, I can quickly shove the briefcase into my backpack and have my arms free as I slide down the wing tip to safety.

On the flip side of the pamphlet, the scene shifts. There the plane, perfectly idle and complacent, floats on the ocean. More yellow equipment comes popping out of cabinets and from under seats: yellow life vests and rubber life rafts. One, two, three - pull the ropes in the direction of the now familiar red arrow, and passengers are effortlessly equipped for the ocean phase.

(I wonder if the red arrows are also marked on the doors, cabinets and rafts, or are the passengers expected to run back to their seats, locate the pamphlets, and follow the pictures in order to get anything to open or inflate?)

The rafts are perfectly suited to water travel. Three are featured filled with survivors. At least twenty people seated shoulder to shoulder, feet touching in the center, fit into a raft. Once everyone is seated, a man confidently cuts a rope and sets the rubber conveyance adrift. It is an orderly scene; the groupings of survivors seem congenial.

The problem is, how can a plane land smoothly on *top* of the ocean? Wouldn't the sleek aerodynamic design work equally well in water so when a plane nose-dives into water, it will plow straight to the depths? Or, when the plane impacts with water, wouldn't the body crumple and the wings detach, wings I am supposed to slide down to safety on?

I have never adequately answered these questions, nor do I know whom to direct them to in order to get answers. Each time I browse through a glossy pamphlet, the same questions arise though the illustrations differ slightly with each aircraft. I've taken a liking to the yellow rafts in the last scene where the plane floats on water. I can even see myself comfortable in a bright yellow raft, confident that my briefcase and papers are safe in the backpack on my shoulders.

Perhaps it's intentional to end a pamphlet on disaster preparations with an upbeat scene. Never mind the improbability of the plane floating languidly *above* water, I tell myself. Rest assured. There *is* room for me in one of the brightly colored yellow inflatables that float freely away from a disabled and deficient aircraft. Most important, I will not be alone; the prospects for companionship are quite favorable.

FIRE IN THE HILLS ABOVE HOME

It is the morning after I eat *lengua Nicaragua* at a Mission district cafe with poets from El Salvador. On the radio, *cantatas español.* This late October morning the sun is so strong I can sit outdoors and drink a cafe latte with my friend Graham at the Hudson Bay Cafe. I love the heat beating off the brick wall behind me, rising from the cement walk under my feet. I roll up my sleeveless top so the sweat on my stomach can dry in the wind. Leaves rustle by scraping the sidewalk. Later I'll remember the wind and the heat. The sky is an intense blue, the air in the East Bay remarkably clear and fresh.

"Let's run away to the beach," I joke to Graham who reads the *New York Times* across the table from me. "Sure," he says, "Whenever you're ready." But I'm the one who can't go.

I have a deadline the next day and at the height of a glorious Indian summer I'm resigned to sit indoors at the computer and work on a writing project.

My house, set beside a tall pine, is dark inside; I need lights in the day to read and work. In the cool dark of my study around noon as I'm working at the computer a wind shakes the pine branches at the side of the house. The wind is so rousing for those few moments I pause to think, With that kind of wind, the beach will be cool. Just as well we didn't go. Now I don't feel like I'm missing out on a great day at the beach, the last hot day of the season, perhaps.

In the middle of the next sentence the sun dims dramatically. Out of the corners of my eyes I sense the sun faltering in the windows behind me. I know without consciously thinking about it how white clouds dim the sun; they softly shield the intense rays. This is a dark screen against a clear brilliant sky. I am drawn outside. There is a black ominous funnel of smoke that rises from a single source up in the hills. Something nasty is burning. I can't see what. The wind sweeps the smoke across the sky, an ugly black river screens the sun.

I walk to the middle of the street and bend down so I can see beneath the trees up to the hills. Fire flares. Open flames appear crimson under black smoke. A number of neighbors come out to watch and stand around in the street. We talk. After eight months I'm still the newcomer to the neighborhood. The fire is close but not close enough to threaten.

I go back indoors but I can't focus on work so I call my son in Sonoma. He is watching the Berkeley fire on the TV.

"TV?" I ask.

"Yeah, it looks pretty bad."

"Water your plants there," I tell him. "There's a fire in Sonoma county, too."

"I've been watering all day," he says.

My daughter is at work but I phone anyway and leave a message on her answering machine. "What do you think of this heat? There's a fire in the hills here. Love you . . ."

I call an old friend in Seattle and settle into a long conversation, erasing the fire from my mind. We've been through a lot this year; preliminary divorce proceedings; searches for jobs, new responsibilities to care for a large family house after the families break apart. We talk for an hour, catching up on our lives, our children, our business ventures, our future plans, ideas to go back to school. Midway in the conversation I turn the TV on and catch glimpses of the fire coverage. Then I hear sirens outside.

"Can you hear the siren?" I ask my friend.

"Yes," she says.

"Ambulances are bringing the burn victims to the hospital a block away. The fire is getting worse."

My housemate walks in and announces, "The neighbors are evacuating."

"I've gotta go. This looks bad."

I watch the news on television. The fire started the day before in the brush outside the Caldicott tunnel that burrows through the East Bay hills. The Fire Department extinguished the flames but this morning some embers still glowed. They doused the smoldering embers with more water; the situation seemed under control. Suddenly the wind, a hot dry north-easterly Santa Ana flared up and fanned the coals. The fire literally exploded in front of the firemen and a television crew who came to cover yesterday's doused fire. The flames swept across the open grass and threatened houses on the hill in two directions.

Scenes on the TV: fire fighters with hoses; chimneys where houses once stood; homeowners hosing their roofs; people on foot outrunning the fire; evacuees in cars packed with belongings inching down a windy hilly street clogged with other cars, fire engines and ambulances; police lines holding back the curious; reporters out of breath, wiping their brows with kerchiefs; soot rising and ash debris falling as far away as San Francicso. Over the bridges special lanes open for firetrucks from Marin, Petaluma, San Jose, Palo Alto, and many other northern California communities.

The Claremont Hotel, a grand old wooden resort at the foot of the Berkeley hills, becomes the rallying point for volunteers and firemen who come to stop the spread of the fire. A row of eucalyptus trees, a highly volatile wood, stands at the eastern edge of the hotel. The hotel residents are evacuated.

Firemen hose down the roof and keep their hoses aimed at the eucalyptus trees.

My house is less than half a mile from the Claremont. The neighborhood to the south of me where I drank a latte with Graham this morning flashes across the TV screen. Behind the word "Rockridge" a sweeping wall of flames. I suddenly think, Where's Graham?

My housemate carries her cello to the car. "This is irreplaceable," she says.

"I know how you feel. I feel like packing too."

Graham calls. He evacuated his home in Rockridge at 4:00. Now he sits in the bar of the Grand Hotel in downtown Oakland watching the fire on the news.

"I tried to phone earlier but the line was busy."

"Did you take anything?" I ask.

"Nothing. I can't deal with packing. I just left. Why don't you come down here? We can watch the fire together."

"I think I will but I need time to think. Call me back."

I rationalize departure: a half mile is not that far away. The radio announcer claims the fire hoses are dry. With no water to fight the fire, there is no way to stop it. Winds gust and fan the flames. The fire is spreading. No one or nothing can halt its voracious consumption. Where houses once stood, the only remains are cement foundations and towering brick chimneys. The irony of hearths without homes. Seemingly indestructible chrome automobile bumpers melt into pools of molten metal. Later explanations will surface: it is the seventh year of the drought and the land is parched, anything will ignite at the slightest provocation; homeowners drained the water supply by squirting their roofs; ten water reservoirs ran dry; fire hoses from different districts didn't connect together so no water could be pumped through the hoses; no one could find the key to the generator to set the pumps going.

A helicopter carries a barrel on a long wire, dips the barrel into Lake Temescal, and carries the water back to the flames. I hear the chop, chop of rotating blades above me in the sky. I know at this point the fire will rage all night. If a fire is headed my way, my mind will be so stirred up I will not be able to sleep. The drama on television is addictive. I listen to the simultaneous broadcasts of radio and television for two hours. I flip the remote and change stations sporadically as if one vision of the disaster isn't enough. The radio commentator at the base of the foothills where the fire rages captures the action at the front lines; his voice is high-strung, tense, almost screaming. I'm exhausted, envisioning disaster.

Aside from the threat of destruction and harm to my body and my belongings, the second reason to flee the house is the smoke. The air is already bad indoors. The flu I had last week still hangs over me. I tie a damp dish towel over my nose and mouth. I don't want to breathe the smoke any more than I have to.

"I'm coming," I tell Graham when he calls back, "but I need an hour. I want to pack some things."

"I'll be here," he says.

My life is not threatened; just my possessions. I have some time. I believe if I evacuate I will have more peace of mind for the next twenty-four hours than if I stay in the fire zone. I remember all the survival pamphlets I've glanced over. Most list food supplies to stock in case of an earthquake when water supplies or power fails. What should I pack? I can pick and chose. I have a car and gas and a friend waiting for me. What's valuable? If the house burns when I'm gone, what will I miss? What do I need to survive after the fire? What is irreplaceable?

At a time of harm and potential loss, it's impossible to think clearly and rationally. My papers, my photograph albums, my books are valuable; money, jewels, appliances, and tools are useful. I rent the house and own no furniture to worry about. Most of my possessions are papers. Suddenly I regret caring for endless scraps and files of paper. If I was a hermit, or lived in a cloister or hermitage, I wouldn't have many possessions and wouldn't face these choices. Why do I need so many papers around? Why can't I just walk away, free and unattached? I vow to reorder my life, my possessions, but there's no time now.

I pack. The first thing I carry to the car is my computer hard drive. All my recent writing for the last year is on the hard drive. I haven't been backing up files onto disks so I have few hard copies. Then I reason I might as well save the laser printer which cost $800 four months ago. Next I pack my journals from the last twenty years, files of unfinished stories, files of story ideas. I can't leave behind files of business stuff: bills, a deed, my divorce papers. The way the documents and bills define my life, my value, my debt, seems important. If I stopped to think I'd realize it's possible to get duplicates of papers, especially bills. But I don't stop. The list grows: a golden statue of the Buddha, videos and tapes of my performance work, the only documentation I have. My housemate and I pass each other on the stairs carrying armfuls of items we treasure.

I don't think about clothes or books. Both are replaceable. My writing, my life's work, is irreplaceable. After this is over I vow to clear out my files; turn the drafts into publishable works. If published then the material will be finalized and preserved without my having to schlep files, manuscripts, and books around with me whenever I move or evacuate from fires, as if the act of evacuation is something I'll be doing again in the near future. If I were famous I could archive my papers somewhere like a library. What a privilege to have librarians organize and store papers for me. "Hey! Stop daydreaming! Get busy packing," I remind myself.

An hour is a luxurious amount of time to pack. A lot can be rescued and crammed into a car in an hour. Still each decision seems hasty. When I finally leave the house and shut the door, I feel as if I'm fleeing a sinking ship.

"Might as well watch the fire from a safe distance," Graham said.

I drive toward downtown Oakland. The smoke in the air is heavy. The black fire cloud wafts south, across the city, following me. Too bad we didn't plan on meeting away from the smoke. There's no escape from the ash and soot. At every cross street people stand on the pavement. All down Telegraph Avenue crowds face the hills, point to the fire. Larger crowds congregate at Lake Merritt. It is a time of community; we communally witness the fire, share in the horror, in the blight we're powerless to stop that scars our neighborhoods. As long as the fire is raging there is a shared fear, a subtle panic, and remorse. Friends, families, strangers - it doesn't matter who we know or don't. Those fighting to save their homes, those fleeing the fire, those taking in the stranded - we are all neighbors. This is our community, our home. We suffer together.

When I see Graham we embrace. "We should head north," I say, "to the coast."

"Sit down," he says. "Relax."

"How?" I ask.

We watch the news on a large TV screen above and behind the bar. That night we sleep on the floor of a friend's home near downtown Oakland. We go to sleep with visions of the fire. During the night soot sneaks through the walls, the windows. The winds, the horrible winds, subside. I stumble out of bed thirsty.

For days the television coverage is nonstop: pictures of flames; the rising death toll; maps of the neighborhoods which burned; interviews with survivors, volunteers, firemen, police. The newspapers run front-page photos, headlines. For the first time I feel part of a national disaster, a front-page feature.

In two days I return home. On the freeway at night my eyes follow a line of twinkling lights denoting houses in the hills, until they go black. My eyes sweep the horizon; black is where the fire destroyed everything. The hills above my home, now a long black void. I feel like a firestorm survivor even though the fire didn't reach my backyard. I feel the remorse of neighbors. It will be a month before I walk in the hills and survey the damage. For now I don't need to see it; the loss is too great, too close to ignore. I fall asleep before I eat.

In the morning I go outside to get the morning paper. Miraculously I still have a morning paper. While thousands have addresses near me, they no longer have homes or mailboxes, cars or kitchens or gardens or manuscripts or food or shelter. The heavy, foggy Berkeley air is saturated with soot. The smell is like a barbecue fire doused with water. When water vaporizes over the hot coals, steam and ash clouds rise up and a pungent aroma of ash carries in the air. The scent brings back another time when I lived in India and cooked all my meals on a charcoal fire. After I cooked, I picked up each piece of charcoal carefully with fire tongs and dunked it into a pan of water. The coals sizzled, slogged, steamed and hissed as the fire gasped a last breath and died. Wood in India is expensive and scarce. Even the slightest black bit of charcoal can reignite and burn.

I feel like I've been facing a firing squad, when the general calls a stop just after the person in front of me is shot. "No more, today," he announces. "You, go back home." I stagger inside. I didn't lose anything in the firestorm. Why do I feel so rotten?

Suddenly I realize my body is talking to me; I'm starving. I bike to the market for food. As if I'm shopping for my first, or last, meal. I crave odd foods, as if I'm seeing produce for the first time after a long ordeal. Sweet red peppers. Corn on the cob. Pomegranates. At home I prepare the peppers with tomatoes from my garden. My fall garden survived the catastrophe; I'm grateful for small comforts. The salad is bright red. Fire foods: red crispy sweet peppers - the juice quenches my throat - bright red tomatoes. The corn I eat is piping hot, so delicious I can't wait until it is cool. I bite into the steaming cob; I crave the heat. It is scrumptiously crunchy, juicy and hot; my tongue burns.

Sheepishly I unpack the car. My hard drive, laser printer, and box of journals go back to the shelves and tables. The hasty packing and evacuation seem so futile now. At the time, the hour I spent packing calmed me in the midst of a siege, helped me feel as if I were accomplishing something, doing something. Moving around felt better than passively watching the fire on the television.

Shuffling papers from car to closet and back again confuses me. Looking at my unpublished manuscripts frustrates me. All this writing work. What good is it? The notebooks and files are dusty, the paper is fading. So many papers take up storage space, fill up shelves and file drawers. When will I complete these manuscripts? The act of uprooting my papers triggered a sense of disruption, not of material belongings, but of a tranquility, a state of mind not threatened by an encroaching fire.

During the seven years I traveled abroad, homelessness was a way of life I chose. From the vantage point of small villages in Asia, when I looked back to my distant home, I felt a longing, a soreness. I didn't want to return home but I missed aspects of home. Longing for home was preferable to being there. I wandered in the way a pilgrim wanders; renouncing the comforts of my original home, traveling the countryside seeking home as a quality of mind; challenging myself to feel at home in any surroundings, in any country or terrain. The fire victims had no choice. The fire descended on them without warning; a few were asleep in bed. Their losses were abrupt and deep. They did not chose displacement; they were innocent victims of a natural disaster. Their plight is a lesson on the nature of impermanence in this life, a reminder of the upheavals that can arise at any moment, a testimonial to the legacy of fire.

Three days later. I wash clothes and hang them in the sun to dry. I notice how much black I wear; the color of mourning. Black pants, black T-shirt; I just bought two black dresses.

Washing and cleaning are cathartic. The sun has shrunk from the hot blasting energy of a Sunday morning a few days earlier to a weak glimmer in the autumn sky. The last hot blast of summer coupled with the fire from nowhere is distant now; yet the pain, the suffering of the victims, will smolder for a long time. When I get dressed, my clothes will be fresh, like new. These domestic rituals comfort me. I am home. I am grateful to be alive.

SHELTER OF BONE, SHELTER OF FLESH

Two hunters trek into the Rockies to retrieve a buck they shot. The buck was too heavy to haul out earlier, so they return in a truck with two horses. Around noon they park the truck by the side of a forest road, mount the horses and follow a trail back into the woods and over a ridge.

They easily locate the spot where they left the buck. With sharp knives the hunters cut the carcass in half, then each straps a section onto one of the horses. Thick, surly clouds eclipse the sun when they set off on the trail back to the road. As they near the seven-thousand-foot ridge, a brisk wind shoves through the branches of the trees and stings their faces. At the top of the ridge winds hurl sleet and the horses rear up in fear.

The hunters halt; snow pellets sting their eyes. Exasperated, they stare out into a fury of white. The winds do not diminish. The force of a blizzard soon rages, obliterating all traces of the trail. The hunters huddle together under a tree, the only shelter they find. Sleet melts on their jackets, and soaks through the woolen fabric; cold seeps into their skin.

In the absence of shelter, all climates are extreme. On the high mountain ridges during a storm the chances of survival are slim without shelter. Blizzards have a life span of their own. During the afternoon the hunters try to light a fire from the twigs and branches they gather, but the wind extinguishes match after match. When night overtakes them, the men shiver uncontrollably; their body temperatures fall dramatically.

The hunters did not bring food. To nourish themselves and fortify their bodies to brave a long night of freezing weather conditions, the hunters untie the buck and slice chunks of the meat. Since there is no fire, they chew the meat raw but the taste of cold deer flesh does little to revive their spirits, energy and body temperature.

When hypothermia sets in, thinking may become irrational. The hunters make plans. Frostbite threatens. They discuss their options. Since the trail is obliterated, locating the road and the truck is impossible in the dark. There is no way to build a fire, since the last match is gone. There is no natural shelter. Their clothes are soggy and damp; already their bodies quake uncontrollably. Huddling together isn't enough to raise their body temperatures, nor can they keep up a frenzied dance and stomp to generate circulation and warmth.

If morning brings a let-up in weather, they can follow the trail and locate the truck. But how to survive the night?

A handful of early pioneers who attempted to cross the Rockies late one fall became stranded. They located shelter, but food rations were in short supply. When the choice of food became less and less desirable, eating became an unpopular necessity. The pioneers needed to locate additional sustenance. A few of the pioneers succumbed; the survivors ate meat from their slaughtered horses. When the horse meat was consumed and there was still no sign of rescue, the choice was between starvation or eating the flesh of another, less fortunate, traveler. Since a few pioneers had already died, the question of murder was thankfully circumvented. The grim reality was: those who ate the flesh of their fellow travelers survived; those who didn't died.

For the hunters stranded on the seven thousand-foot ridge in a blizzard, the question of food is not as urgent as the question of warmth. As hypothermia sets in for men and horses alike, the hunters secretly covet the animals for the warmth their bodies might provide. Death is imminent for men and horses alike, yet there is a chance the horses can provide an added warmth that will enable the hunters to stave off death for a few more hours.

The horses whine and paw the ground; one tries to break away but fails; they feel the cold chill but are helpless to fight it. The hunters think if they kill the horses they will alleviate the discomfort and pain. At nine p.m., unable to face the grim task of killing their own animals, they shoot each other's horse.

The hunters snuggle up to and against the bodies. Their hands are so numb with cold they can barely grasp their hunting knives. First one hunter slits his horse's belly, guts the innards, and hollows a nest in the rib cage.

"Do it," he commands his friend. "Just do it. Like I did. Slit the belly, go on. Do it."

Spastic with the abrasive cold, they each climb inside the hollow cave of a horse's belly and pull the carcass back over them like a massive, pulsating blanket.

What is the temperature of a horse's belly? How long will a slaughtered horse retain body heat? A few hours, all night? In the shelter of flesh, as the hunters crouch in silence, their bodies absorb the warmth of blood and gut. Huddled inside the carcasses, the hunters struggle alone. One thinks of his wife and children; the other mourns his horse, his companion for many seasons. At least there is warmth, the bloody chambers seal off the cold.

After two hours they need to stretch and pee. Even though the outside temperature assaults their bodies with numbing cold, they leave the confines of flesh. They open the carcasses, and climb out, shutting behind them the gaping hole in an attempt to preserve every iota of the rapidly diminishing heat. By two a.m. the dead horses no longer steam with heat; the slabs of flesh turn clammy and threatening.

The hunters survive the next four hours by a combination of persistence, wits, luck and the solace of friendship. With a fear of impending death, each nags the other. Delirious and shaking with cold, they stumble down the mountain in the earliest glimmer of light. After one wrong turn, they locate the trail to the road.

"The truck. We're almost there," one shouts. As they race over the last yards of snow, one stumbles; the other drags him to his feet. The driver fumbles momentarily with the key in the frozen lock. Once inside the truck, they laugh a crazy drunken laugh and sigh the relief of those who battle death and win. The shortest way back to warmth and shelter is straight down the road which they came on. As they drive in silence, the truck heater spurts wild gusts of hot, noisy air.

WHALES TRAPPED IN THE ICE

A Point Barrow hunter named Aiyu first spots the whales trapped in the ice. It is late fall. His village is the northernmost town in Alaska. There is only twenty feet of open water for the whales to breath. The whales take turns lifting their huge barnacle-encrusted snouts up out of the water. The hole will get smaller. There is no turning back the ice. Already the ice pack is five inches deep, too thick for the gray whales to rear up and break through the crust to swim back to open sea.

The village elders talk about the whales but no one knows how to help them. A five inch layer of ice is too thin for anyone to walk on; too thin to venture very far out on the frail ice sheet. A photographer uses a telephoto lens to shoot one of the whales as it rears up out of the water to breath. He wires the photo to a newspaper in Seattle which runs the image on the front page.

Other papers publish the photo. Across the country readers sympathize with the stranded creatures who battle against the inevitable encroaching winter. The plight of the endangered whales competes with stories of murder and bank robberies. Before two weeks pass other local villagers and an assortment of well-intentioned experts descend on Point Barrow in great numbers. There are plans for a rescue operation.

A biologist arrives followed by representatives of environmental groups who camp on the ice. Two villagers, the biologist and three volunteers take turns walking out on the now harder ice sheet to hack at the ice enclosing the small airhole. With simple ice picks and a chain saw, they keep the airhole from freezing over. Day by day, however, the ice grows thicker. One whale shows signs of pneumonia and all three sport cuts and scars where their rough-skinned snouts rear up against the jagged ice in desperate attempts to breath. The whales are exhausted too, from swimming against the ocean current to remain at a strategic distance from the airhole.

Commercial oil companies, hoping to create favorable humanitarian publicity to counteract the inevitable environmental haphazards of their business, join the rescue attempts by donating additional chain saws. Inupiat Eskimo whalers use the new chain saws to carve holes in the ice. Every seventy-five yards they carve a new hole. The whalers, by cutting the airholes in a line, hope to lure the whales to travel, airhole by airhole, back out to open sea.

At the time the whalers begin sawing, the ice measures a foot thick and the growing number of spectators — environmentalists, Inupiat Eskimos, photographers and journalists — are able to stand safely at the edge of the ice hole and reach out and pat the battered whales, as if this gesture might lessen their suffering.

Newspapers carry the daily progress of the whale rescue. Office workers in San Francisco, dock workers in Boston, chicken farmers in Alabama and beauty parlor operators in Miami commiserate with the poor stranded creatures who day by day fight a losing battle with nature. Miraculously the President calls to pep up sagging spirits. The U.S. army is offering the use of a one hundred and eighty-five ton barge, he says, to carve open a forty-foot path for the whales to swim to open water. The hitch is the army stores the barge two hundred miles away in Prudhoe Bay, across the Arctic Ocean ice. It will take some time to get the barge close enough to help the trapped whales.

Nevertheless the army dispatches two helicopters to tow the barge using an eight hundred foot steel cable. The towed barge makes little progress cutting through the ice the first day so workers stay up half the night to empty excess fuel from the overweight barge. They decrease the weight of the barge by an incredible seventy tons and try again the next day.

Back at the rescue camp doubts surface. The helicopter costs up to three thousand dollars an hour to operate, so the price tag for this rescue operation soon reaches five hundred-thousand dollars whether or not the mission succeeds. One helicopter pilot expresses his doubts. In order for the helicopters to tow the heavy barge, the low altitude and angles of pull make the copters vulnerable if the eight hundred foot cable snaps. "The nose is down," the pilot says, "if the line snaps and comes back up to the rotors, we've got real trouble."

Meanwhile scores of suggestions from newspaper readers all over the world pour into the rescue camp. "Use explosives," one reader writes. "Bowling balls flung onto the ice will break it up," another suggests. "Use nets to catch the whales and transport them out of the threatened area," yet another writes.

One man from Minnesota recommends a de-icing machine from his father's factory in the midwest. The machines, popular in Minnesota to keep marinas from freezing over in the winter, utilize large propellers to keep the water churning. The movement inhibits the ice from coalescing. After the rescue team rejects his offer, on his own initiative and expense, the man flies up to Point Barrow undertaking the arduous task of transporting six new de-icing machines which he brings with him.

By this time, the ice surrounding the original hole solidifies enough to support the weight of pick-up trucks and snowmobiles. Curious whale hunters surround the ice hole in snowmobiles, beam their headlights on "bright," and illuminate the night for the Minnesota man as he hooks up his de-icing machines. After the de-icing machines whirr up the slush in the original airhole, they move to the other holes sawed by the whalers at convenient intervals in the direction of open sea, now five miles away.

National Guardsmen armed with high-powered rifles stand by and discourage any curious polar bears who might amble into the vicinity looking for fishing holes. The environmentalists question the logic of subduing and possibly harming one species, the polar bear, in an attempt to rescue another, the California gray whale. Luckily the bears show no interest in the fracas; no rifles fire.

Animal behavior experts join the ad hoc rescue team and offer their opinions. One claims that the whales can survive several more weeks despite their battered condition. "They can bleed a barrel and still be fine," he says. Another expert reasons that since whales normally resurface once every four minutes, the whales are under extreme stress and on the verge of collapse since they now resurface every two minutes. One scientist counters with the suggestion that the whales surface so often because they are enamored with the buzzing of the de-icing machines. Another claims the whales like the hum of the chain saw. One skeptic says the species will be better off without the three stragglers who obviously have faulty tracking mechanisms that disoriented them so easily in the first place.

Updates on the progress of the helicopter-towed barge filter back to the rescue camp. After another day the barge travels a total of only six miles. At that slow pace, spring will arrive before the barge smashes through the remaining two hundred miles of ice. A spokeswoman berates the hostile conditions. "A shallow sandy area and a covering of brittle old ice is inhibiting the barge," she apologizes.

Rescuers initiate another plan. They agree to use a discarded five-ton hammer with a sharp tip, once used in the construction of the Alaska oil pipeline. A helicopter transports the hammer, nicknamed "crusher" and "bullet," also from Prudhoe Bay. In ball and chain style, men riding in the helicopter drop and redrop the hammer onto the ice. They follow each punch with twenty minutes of additional blows to create holes twenty to thirty feet wide. They punch holes every one hundred feet. Rescuers play tape-recorded voices of killer whales to frighten the whales and encourage them to follow the airholes out to open sea.

To ensure pounding on the ice wouldn't frighten the whales, the helicopter begins the airborne assault where the ice sheet meets open sea, and moves inland, punching holes along the way. Volunteers on the ice pack, perhaps discouraged with yet another story of exotic equipment en route to the barren and inaccessible area, and perhaps anxious to just keep their limbs moving to ward off the cold, continue to carve out holes with hand-held equipment. They rejoice on the eve of the first day of busting ice holes after the whales move to the twenty-fourth hole. But at one hundred feet between holes, the distance the whales cover amounts to only a half mile; there are four and a half miles to go.

Meanwhile an environmental group in contact with a Soviet icebreaker three hundred miles away reports that the Russians are considering joining the rescue. Hopes again surge.

Americans frequently stage massive rescue operations to save troubled whales. When endangered whales inexplicably beach themselves on both the east and west coasts, rescuers successfully nudge, coax and lift many of the inert weighty creatures back out to sea again. The public easily sympathizes when these highly intelligent mammals cast themselves up on a beach in a mysterious massive stranding. Color television flashes the daily drama of the trapped California gray whales. Volunteers reach out and stroke the gigantic, sorrowful heads. Footage of the huge whale snouts, surfacing so close to human contact, in a cramped hole surrounded by inhospitable and impenetrable ice, mesmerizes viewers in living rooms, hotels and bars across America.

Animal welfare activists applaud the outpouring of sympathy, but are quick to put in plugs for other, less popular but equally tormented animals. "Pigs," one advocate suggests, "are lovely, very interesting and intelligent animals. But they don't get any attention at all."

Sociologists wonder: Why whales? Why not an equal concern for the homeless humans stranded on the streets and alleys of major cities across the nation?

In the end, the Soviet icebreaker, contacted again, this time by the U.S. government, agrees to proceed to Point Barrow and carve a channel for the whales to swim to freedom. The icebreaker easily opens a path through thickening ice. A hundred people gather to watch and help. They cheer as the surviving two whales—the third whale fails to surface and is presumed dead—follow the ice breaker as it heads out the channel. The cheers are short-lived, however, because the next morning the whales only cover a mile and a half and the chunks of ice in the fifteen-below-zero temperature start to refreeze and close the newly opened channel.

Rescuers convene and agree to use recordings to lure the whales down the channel to open sea so they can continue their migration south. This time they reject recordings of killer whales; the sound might frighten the already disoriented creatures. One environmentalist claims whales love new age guitar music. The rescuers agree on the one sound that the whales associate with safety—the music of the buzzing chain saws. As a back-up rescuers order an amphibious tractor to aid in grinding up chunks and slush but the tractor is not needed as the whales are charted the next day, swimming in open sea.

INTRUSIONS IN ICE
A Sequence of Nineteen Tales

In the early 1800's, a Mr. Frederick Tudor successfully exported ice from New England. He shipped a total of four thousand three hundred and fifty-two tons of ice from Fresh Pond, Cambridge to Havana, Cuba and other southern ports in 1832. He cut the ice blocks from the surface of rented ponds, insulated the ice with non-conducting materials such as sawdust and hay, and stored the ice in immense ice houses. The ice then traveled by horse wagons to shipping vessels bound for foreign markets.

In spite of the costs of sawing, splitting, lifting and towing large blocks of ice together with the costs of storage and transportation, the ice trade prospered. In Calcutta and China the American ice sold for two cents a pound. Even though the ice shipped from America traveled such a great distance, still the cost was half the price of local varieties of ice.

In India English entrepreneurs developed an indigenous method for harvesting ice. When the December temperatures dropped enough to induce water to freeze, the operations of the ice pits began. The ice pits consisted of thousands of earthen pots, set in rows and insulated in shallow beds with sugar cane leaves, rice straw or grass. By keeping the shallow beds perfectly dry to produce evaporation, the water froze in the clay pots overnight.

To operate the ice production, on a crisp evening with a frosty edge in the air, the ice-makers beat on hand drums to signal the coolies in the bazaar to come to the ice pits. Hundreds of coolies, men, women and children, filled every ten-inch-wide pot with water from large water canisters. At three a.m. the chief ice-maker checked the pots. If the surface contained an inch or two of solid ice, he sounded the drum again, this time to call the coolies back to harvest the ice. The coolies knocked the ice out of the pots with long-handled tools, and scooped the chunks into laundry-sized baskets. When the baskets filled, the coolies carried them on their heads to a central ice-house and tossed the contents into a great pit.

Inside the pit, men draped in blankets for warmth, wore shoes and carried huge wooden mallets. They beat the harvested ice into a hard, flat mass. To keep the ice cool, they covered the pounded ice blocks with mats and straw. They collected ice in this fashion, inches at a time, from December until early March. The ice houses opened for business in the beginning of May. After a good harvest, the supply lasted the local British community until the middle of August.

Although the Himalayas, source of countless glaciers, were far closer than New England, no merchants undertook the job of harvesting glacial deposits and transporting the bulk back down to the plains. The indigenous ice harvested from the ice pits and beaten into a mass dissolved more rapidly than the frozen pond ice from America. The superior ice, the merchants conceded, was the American ice.

*

Language confirms a knowledge of ice. Readers who marvel at descriptions of snow cultures with their abundant snow vocabularies, assume a vocabulary of ice and snow does not exist in the English language. This is only partly true. English lexicons provide many words depicting the textures, movements and accumulations of ice and snow. *Frost, icicle, slush, sleet, hail, glacier, floe,* and *iceberg* appear as everyday colloquial expressions. *Growler, rime, glaze, permafrost,* and *bergy bits* are less common as are *iceblink, ice field, ice shelf, ice sheet, ice cap,* and *ice foot,* though each defines, in plain English terminology, distinct icy conditions.

Other words depicting formations in ice are borrowed from other languages, yet listed in English dictionaries: *sastruga, polynya, neve, firn, serac, moulin, crevasse,* and *graupel.* The existing words in English, including terms borrowed from other languages not necessarily the languages of arctic cultures, comprise a terminology of ice that is actually quite extensive. In addition, the terms often reflect an intimate knowledge of unusual patterns and behavior of ice.

Serac and *moulin*, for example, are terms borrowed from the French language. The words have other meanings besides those referring to conditions located within a glacier. Perhaps the ice definitions are only the third or fourth in a list of usages. Specifically, *serac* and *moulin* refer to conditions located within a crevice of a glacier. *Serac* is a pinnacle; whereas *moulin* is the crevasse itself, or the actual vertical shaft or cavity. I'm reminded of Toulouse-Lautrec's painting "Le Moulin Rouge" where leggy Parisian nightclub dancers kick up their skirts and ruffled petticoats, toes in the air over their heads, a scene of gaiety and pomp. To add *rouge* to *moulin* adds warmth, a blush, color to an otherwise colorless crevasse.

Moulin also depicts the way the crevasse was formed, that is, by the slow seepage of surface water falling through a crack. This dripping water cuts through the ice like a rotating blade. That is why the image of a mill, a device that perpetuates a repetitive action, stimulated early glaciologists to apply the French word for mill, i.e. *moulin*, to the eroding crevasse.

To mill also means to move in a circle, to swirl in an eddying mass. The word windmill conjures up both the graceful revolution of sails in the wind, as in wind curtains, and at the same time the grinding of the millstone inside the mill, pulverizing the grains, eroding a solid mass by constant friction.

*

The movement of glaciers was not discovered until 1861. Early geologists were correct in classifying glaciers as metamorphic rock, but as with other rock surfaces, glaciers were assumed to be stationary. As it happened, a climbing party led by a Dr. Hamel was swept away by an avalanche on the Glacier de Bossons, on Mount Blanc in Switzerland. The party was lost at an altitude of fourteen thousand, seven hundred and eighty-four feet in the year 1820.

Ordinarily the white on white, the melting and retreating process associated with glaciers is difficult to witness. But forty-one years after the tragedy, the remains of Dr. Hamel's team clearly turned up at the snout of the glacier, that is, at four thousand, four hundred feet.

Calculations were made: If the total descent was ten thousand, three hundred and eighty-four feet in forty-one years, the descent per annum was ten thousand, three hundred and eighty-four divided by forty-one, that is, two hundred and fifty-three feet per year or, an incredible eight and a half inches a day.

*

Sporadic and unusual snow or ice falls have been recorded throughout recent history. One Florida zookeeper, after a freak snow, plugged in sun lamps to counteract a deleterious chill that threatened the resident iguana population.

After a ferocious blizzard snow drifts inundated a city in upstate New York. To clean up, the mayor engaged gondola cars to transport some of the excess ice and snow to southern climes where melting would transpire at an innocuous rate, and provide needed moisture to towns with limited precipitation.

In Yugoslavia blocks of ice weighing from three hundred and thirty to four hundred and forty pounds apiece, rained down with great force on the tiny village of Resnik. The smashing produced an awesome roaring.

"The blocks took a couple of days to melt completely," a frightened farmer explained, "and small craters were left in the soil."

Experts proposed two theories to explain the phenomena: a secret ice bombing by UFO's; or the natural ice collection on wing tips of commercial airliners suddenly dislodged over the area. But blocks of ice weighing over four hundred pounds? How many wing tips would it take to account for the rainlike effect? Aviation authorities later discounted the airliner theory since no flights were scheduled over the village at the time of the ice fall. The investigating director concluded with unscientific brevity, "We are completely baffled by this."

*

A geologic film crew traveled to the Cascade mountain range to film an avalanche in slow motion, and chart patterns, routes and behavior of shifting snow. As the photographer set up his camera and tripod downhill and away from the path of the intended avalanche, two others walked to a nearby ridge, discharged guns and yahooed in unison. When their ruckus failed to trigger a loosening of snow, they ignited sticks of dynamite.

This worked. The snow was dislodged. The ensuing snowballing wall not only roared towards the camera but quickly overpowered the photographer, intently peering through his frost-resistant lens.

The film that was retrieved when his body was dug out from under thirty feet of snow is valuable today in beginning geology classes since it depicts accretion in snow walls: an enormous icy mass billows like a mushroom-shaped cloud yet moves full speed ahead until the entire screen is so white it blacks out.

*

Certain beasts inhabit snowy regions: snow leopards and polar bears are two varieties. Snow leopards stalk smaller animals which nest and burrow in ice. The bears fish Arctic seas. These predators skillfully eke out an existence in frozen wastelands and frigid waters. They thrive where, over the years, others failed. Witness the stilled and stuffed replicas of woolly mammoths which haunt the icy chambers of science museums.

In Tibet, an abominable snowman, or *yeti,* is rumored to survive in icy regions at very high altitudes. Prints, more footlike than paw, by this two-legged creature link the beast to man, another two-legged creature. Since the prints are located in snow, the term "snowman" seems logical. But over the years the adjective "abominable" has been linked with this unknown snow creature. Considering the miracle of survival in an icy clime, the term "abominable" seems unreasonable. Isn't survival itself a cause for marvel?

Some rumors persist to account for such a loathsome description. The depth of print, for example, is an indication of an immense, weighty being. Perhaps obesity is a reason for the derisive term. Of course hairiness, an undesirable characteristic associated with beasts, assures the creature the necessary warmth needed to survive in subzero weather. But what distinguishes a healthy coat of fur from an overgrown, shaggy, matted skin? Is length or unevenness of hair an abomination?

Or, consider the prints: longish, a recognizable heel and toes. Are the footprints overly broad, flat, huge, pigeon-toed or otherwise deformed or ugly?

Shrieks have been reported. Feces photographed. But is an eerie cry abominable? Is one feces specimen more odious than another? Since heat conducts and ripens odors, frozen turds probably do not even stink.

The beast must prey on other creatures since no plants grow in icy altitudes to support a herbivore. Is fear the abomination? Fear of some weighty, shaggy, clumsy, fleeting—since none have been captured, killed or retrieved—carnivore?

*

Two factors contribute to the natural mobility of ice: water currents and gravity. Polar water currents move free-floating ice masses. The force of gravity accounts for both avalanches and the downward slide of glaciers, that is, the perpetual creep of glacial deposits.

The mobility of ice excels in Arctic environments. At sea there is *drifting ice, ice fields,* and *ice floes* or *floebergs.* These are divided by size. Giant floes range from two to ten kilometers long; medium-large, five hundred to two thousand meters; medium-small, one hundred to five hundred meters; and the small floes, twenty to one hundred meters in length. Smaller sizes are categorized as *blocks, ice cakes, sludge,* and *brash.* Ice that was once mobile is classified according to the loss of mobility: *grounded floe, beached shore ice, ice foot, grounded sea ice, grounded hummock, shore ridge of stranded ice.*

The International Ice Patrol monitors the international ocean shipping lanes, scouting for ominous ice masses. If one is located, military planes may bomb the huge frozen interlopers to reduce their size and threat.

Where was the Ice Patrol the night the *Titanic* collided with a drifting berg and sank on its maiden voyage?

*

In the hierarchy of ice terminology, *brash* has little status. *Brash* is a nautical term for small fragments of crushed ice, swept ashore by the wind or water currents. Perhaps it is because *brash* is crushed and of indeterminate size and shape, a haphazard of semifrozen water, that the ice loses its distinct sharp edge, like ice at the bottom of a soft-drink cup after the drink is consumed. This softening must account for the term *brash*, a term that can also mean, when applied to behavior, impertinence, rashness or impudence.

Sludge, like *brash*, because of the mixture of water and ice, has inferior associations. Mud, mire, ooze and slush, like *sludge*, are equally "bottom of the barrel." This is predictable if you consider the combination of the letters *s* and *l* plus either an *o* or a *u*. Not one word that begins with these combinations of letters has a reputable connotation. Consider: slob, slobber, slog, slop, slope, slosh, sloth, slough, sloven, slow, slow-witted, slug, sluggish, slum, slumber, slur and slut. The evidence is overwhelming.

When ice is isolated into fragments as in *brash* or *sludge*, the vulnerability accounts for the lower status. Ice that asserts its dominion over water, that is, ice in solid blocks and chunks, is far superior.

*

Ice can be distinguished by age, whereas water cannot. The proximity of water to its watershed might be a gauge of purity by distance, but not age. When glacial movement ceases, the history of the motion is preserved in ice, sometimes carved in rock. Hoary is a colloquial way to describe age; grayhaired and wizened when applied to a man. But in the terminology of ice, *hoar frost* is fresh and young. Other forms of young ice: *pancake ice, brackish ice crust, ice rind, early winter ice,* and *thick winter ice. Polar ice* is ice that has maintained its form and solidity for over two years.

*

A company in Seattle recently transported blocks of manufactured ice to Alaska. Why Alaska, the source of countless manifestations and accumulations of ice?

The sponsors of an Alaskan arts festival needed large blocks of ice for an annual ice-carving event. To festival organizers, clarity was worth the price of shipping. Artificially frozen ice is clearer and freer of sediment than ice found in natural states. Artists preferred the commercially produced ice with the higher degree of transparency.

When Mr. Tudor, the first exporter of ice in the 1800's, first shipped his product, the phenomenon of consumer ice was unprecedented in southern countries. Now only rare ice with purported efficacious qualities is exported from one region to another. Pre-pollution era ice from glacial caches in Greenland, for example, are sold in department stores in Manhattan. The one hundred-thousand year old Greenland ice demonstrates a superior 'staying power.' When the ice melts, crackling noises accompany the release of air compressed for thousands of years. The price for thirty-five ounces is seven dollars.

The Japanese also import ice from Greenland. The ice, aged and pure, is claimed to be a cure-all for hangovers. Consequently imported Greenland ice is available in Tokyo cocktail lounges and bars at inflated prices.

*

Other recent events have spurred entrepreneurs to engage in the transportation of large masses of ice. Moving ice over land is cumbersome and expensive, but one seven-ton chunk was flown from Alaska to Washington, D.C. by commercial airliner so crowds at a folklife festival could mill around and experience an Arctic spectacle in the middle of a humid Washington summer.

Prince Mohammed Faisal of Saudi Arabia is the founder of Iceberg Transport International, a company which proposes to tow icebergs to arid countries. The prince is convinced that towing icebergs is cheaper than producing water by desalinization. To tow the bergs, he explains, technicians in the Antarctic would first shape a large ice mass into a boatlike form, then wrap it in plastic and sailcloth to prevent severe melting. A tugboat would tow the enormous package to the desert regions of the Middle East. Even though the entire trip may take from six to twelve months traveling at one knot per hour, calculations estimate there would still be enough ice left to melt for drinking water if the original block weighed a minimum of a hundred million tons.

*

Mirage, though an ephemeral, visual phenomenon, can be scientifically classified as "superior" or "inferior." Mirages in ice are "superior" to those produced by other conditions such as the mirages in a hot or humid environment.

In the dictionary, *fata morgana* appears between fate and fatal. This superior image, as it were, is confined by fate and death. If the superiority of these *fata morganas* is explained by larger and more realistic images, the illusion is one of grandeur. In terms of vision and ice, "grand" may imply greatness, but to the point of fatality, or extreme disillusionment.

Robert E. Peary, en route to the North Pole, confidently named a series of ice peaks rising in the distance, Crocker Land. Subsequent efforts to find and locate the mountain range, however, have proved fruitless or fatal. The peaks, rising deftly between the horizon and the sky, were grand figments of an hallucination of ice, or one of the more concrete examples of a superior mirage, a *fata morgana.*

*

To animate a substance, or to describe an inanimate substance in animated terminology, is fairly common. *Snow eater,* for example, is a gusting wind that has a warm temperature. The blowing appears to melt, or eat snow. *Granular,* a term to describe variations of frozen precipitations and *graupel,* a term for snow pellets, as well as *corn snow, spilled oats* and *rice clusters,* add to an illusion of consumption.

Nieve penitente is another example of an animated structure in snow. In this case the characteristic form of a kneeling penitent is equated with a certain top-heavy accumulation of snow. When the ground is warmer than the air, irregular melting of snow from the ground up produces mushroom shapes. The small base and top-heavy umbrella give the illusion of kneeling human figures, snow pilgrims, *nieve penitentes*, frozen in prayer.

Being implies motion; motion implies being. Movement as in *ice falls* or *avalanches* determines a behavior, a pattern of motion. All living things move, if not externally, then always internally. A *galloping glacier* is a glacier that retreats or advances with great speed, like a mustang, covering a kilometer a day or more.

What about the reverse? It is also common to use inanimate qualities—geologic or climatic in terms of ice—to describe a person. For example, "her veins became iced," "her smile broke the ice," "cold shoulders" and "the tip of the iceberg." Ice in terms of behavior is descriptive of undesirable situations or reactions. Expressions such as "cut no ice" or "on thin ice" further allude to defeatist or precarious predicaments. Even snow as an adjective or verb as in "a snow job" or to be "snowed under," implies deceit, sham, or an overabundance to the point of fatality.

*

The Riverside Ice Company located in southern California pioneered the use of commercial ice to create snowy winter scenes for snow-craving residents of that hot, dry, dusty region.

On a typical December day, in a quiet town on the Mohave desert, a truck from the company pulls up in front of a home at nine a.m. carrying twenty three-hundred-pound blocks of ice. The attendant inside the truck shaves the ice with a large machine and spurts the small bits across the homeowner's lawn through a large nozzle. In less than an hour, five tons of *snow* dust the house and lawn, transforming the landscape into a winter wonderland. Never mind the blooming roses and the desert palms. Without rain, the *snow* lasts three days in seventy-degree weather.

December is the busiest month. Orders come in from sixty miles away. Even though the fine snow pellets have the texture of the snow packed into snow cones rather than real snow, jubilant parents vie to purchase a five-hundred-dollar white Christmas for their family. Lovers want to surprise their mates.

Most winters the company is booked through the current Christmas season but patrons can still order six thousand pounds of sprayed ice over their crabgrass or rockeries to brighten New Year's Day or Valentine's Day.

*

TV snow appears after a television station has gone off the air. Late at night a geometric pattern enclosing the TV station number appears behind a familiar blur of tiny dots or asterisks. After the test pattern is shut off, the final image or broadcast is not a concrete image, but a blur of snowy static. Even the noise resembles a blizzard. The sound, more than the visual flurry, is grating and harsh, an irritating intrusion. But with the volume turned low, the TV snow, the pulsing dots and white flecks, is mesmerizing.

*

The word *debacle* is derived from the French, *debacler*, "to unbar," or "clear" and the latin word *baculum*, "stick" or "rod." Although in common colloquial usage a *debacle* is a collapse or sudden overthrow of order in a political or social setting, a *debacle* is also a technical term for the breaking up of ice in a river.

Witness a *debacle.* Early prospectors in Alaska were the first to bet on when the Tanana River ice floes would break up and begin moving downstream, usually in early May. Recently, more than one hundred thousand tickets were sold in the seventieth annual Nenana Ice Classic, a festival surrounding this seasonal event.

When a river cracks up, the *ice crust* explodes; *icequakes* and *ice collapse* accompany the jarring of floes. To measure the moment of the breakage, enormous logs are fastened into a tripod on the frozen Tanana river. A string connects the logs to a clock on shore, so when the logs tumble they trigger the stopwatch. The tickets indicate the exact moment the ice will break up. Last year nine bettors who guessed the day and minute of the breakup won over fourteen thousand dollars apiece.

*

The pictogram for snow, that is, the Meteorological symbol, is a six-pointed star, suggestive of a single flake. Asters, the daisy-like flowers, and asterisks, the typographical symbol, are also six-pointed. On a typewritten page an asterisk may indicate a heightened awareness. That is, the readers' attention is drawn to what follows or precedes.

The asterisk can also indicate an omission, something that is left out and may be printed at the bottom of the page. Hence, the asterisk might be a sign to look below. Some asterisks indicate "doubtful matter." It is curious that the same symbol calls attention to a heightened awareness, doubtful matter, or an omission.

An asterisk is perhaps the most potent diacritical mark on a typewriter. To comprehend the meaning, consider the context, its placement in a sentence or at the end of a passage. Asterisks, like snowflakes, are mobile.

Asterisks between paragraphs, or at the end or a chapter, indicate a passage of time, a finality.

*

I remember a visit to the zoo. "Do not feed the Animals," warned signs outside the primate area.

Mother looked at the sign, sighed and looked at me. "Ice isn't food," she announced. "What's water anyway . . . what harm is a little water?"

Of course I agreed.

We snatched ice cubes from our waxed-paper soft-drink cups and took turns throwing cubes into the cage. Our noses pressed the chain-link wire fence.

A monkey spotted the glistening white chunks, and swooped down from his branch. Singling out a piece of ice, he picked it up, sniffed, and popped the ice into his mouth.

What did the monkey think of the ice as it melted into not much more than saliva? Do monkeys have saliva? Did he feel the cold? Do monkeys shiver?

As quickly as he popped the cubes into his mouth, they melted into nothingness. The monkey grew perplexed. He tested the cubes, shoved them around, sniffing, batting the ice back and forth between his hands.

When all the ice had melted, he looked up as if to ask us, "What, no more?"

*

There are no vehicles in Tibet. There are wheels but no vehicles. The wheels revolve from the movement of fire, water, and air. Wheels are three-dimensional canisters stuffed with prayers and relics like a Buddha's tooth. For every revolution of a prayer-wheel, each prayer inside—there are said to be thousands—is believed to be recited. To harness the elements of fire, water and air or wind to produce good karma by reciting prayers is more useful than any vehicular transportation. The wheels, for the Tibetans, are better used in praying than in moving carts or wagons along bumpy mountain paths.

There are *yogas*, physical maneuvers and practices in Tibet, special powers that, if developed, may enable one to move very rapidly over the surface of the earth in a type of speed walking, or flying. Perhaps this explains the absence of vehicles. If every Tibetan practiced speed walking, vehicles would just get in the way. Besides, vehicles take up road space and are costly to operate. Vehicles cannot negotiate the high mountain passes. Consider the price of a gallon of gasoline carried by pack mule to the Tibetan plateau.

None of the *yogas*—i.e., dream *yoga*, breath *yoga*, body *yoga*, etc.—are practiced or learned for the sake of business or pleasure. Does that mean the Tibetans are not playful? All work is holy work, the scriptures say, but is there no holy play?

Likewise there are no winter sports in Tibet. No ice-skating or bobsledding, no skiing or cross-country sleighing. Is it because Tibetans face such hardships in day-to-day life in a snowbound country that they take no pleasure in winter sports?

THE RAIN GARAGE

For a sum drivers may pass through the rain garage. The building is open on two sides like a tunnel to allow cars to pass through. No mountains tower above.

Vehicles enter single file. Once inside there is no reverse. Furious inner weather rips and roars as if an entire season of monsoons is captured between the two walls and roof.

Captive like a shoe under a shoeshine boy's buffer, drivers are accosted by an abrasive, brute intensity. Nozzles blast. Electrified jets with more force than waterfalls squirt and batter.

A chaos of spouts shoots an abundance of green foam. Giant mops with long, plastic strands bristle back and forth, swirling and snarling with the gusts of hurricanes.

As abruptly as the rains begin, they cease. A giant, hideous mouth with some crazy appetite slurps up foaming bubbles. Winds, shrieking and yowling, threaten to bust apart the very walls that enclose them.

The exit appears, slowly expanding as the car is pulled through the rain garage. There is no steering. In the rear view mirror the shrieking and yowling slowly recede into the distance and the weather once again appears bright and inviting.

WET BABIES

Frequently I walk down city alleys where cars park, garbage sits and kids toss frisbees back and forth. Once on a walk down an alley behind a church, I noticed windows at the ground level. Squinting, my hand raised to my brow to block the sun, I could see the miniature tables and chairs of a day-care center inside. It was deserted. Maybe it was a Saturday, I forget now, or maybe the children were in the playground at the side of the church. But, no, it was too quiet for that.

The window sills of the day-care center formed a shoulder-high ledge where supplies were stored. There were boxes of toys lining the ledge, out of reach of small hands. A sign on one of the boxes had "a.m. play" printed in green crayon. The box must have been twisted around from its normal position since I was able to read the sign from the alley. The day-care attendants were familiar, no doubt, with what toys were what, since they were clearly distinguishable in the boxes. Any sign at all, in fact, seemed superfluous.

Such order intrigues me. To play cars in the morning, or war or house, but not in the evening . . . or was it war in the afternoon and house in the evening? To play or not to play . . . as if there were a time or season for trucks, tanks or blocks. And what *day*-care center would even be open at night, that is, why distinguish an a.m from a p.m. if there are no p.m. activities?

Another box was labeled "wet babies." It contained a pile of naked, rubber plastic dolls. The pink colors were livelier than life, something like strawberry ice cream or bubble gum. The hard plastic legs were molded in a bent fashion to enable the baby to sit up.

A wet baby, you'd think, would have something to do with layettes, wading pools, and, of course, diapers. I picture babies splashing in pools, sandpails full of water overturned on heads, bathwater kicked out of the layette, and soggy diapers drooping from bottoms. Babies are born wet; they drool, suck, cry, and pee. There are many ways for a baby to be wet. Wetness is implicit in the word baby.

But these dolls are dry. The "wet" of the sign does not describe the state or condition of these babies. Rather it describes their primary function, that is, their ability to dribble moisture from their crotches.

Only in play is wet preferable to dry. To a parent a dry baby is the ideal. An abundance of baby products on the market confirms this: powders, disposable diapers, rubber pants and liners. But in play, the wetness is exciting; water travels from faucet to toy bottle to baby's mouth and out again via a trim, circular hole. The same plastic mold that dimples the bubble-gum-tinted legs also shapes a trim, circular hole, no wider than an eyedropper's.

To play mother or father or doctor is to assert a knowledge beyond experience. Knowing the reason to fill the bottle (the baby is hungry or the baby is crying); knowing how to fill the bottle and where to put it (in the baby's mouth); knowing how to recapture the contents of the bottle (in the diapers) certifies that the caretaker of the plastic baby has mastered this obvious, vital bodily function. This is no small feat. And it is with pride that one child may show another how the process goes.

You can also bathe the baby; I have done it. The water seeps into the arm and leg joints until the insides fill up. Then when you squeeze the stomach, a stream of water and hopefully a gushing noise bursts from the hole. When the mechanics of diapering are mastered, and the process has been replayed to tedium, this gushing stream is highly satisfying. Even in play one needs variations.

The carton piled high with "wet babies" speaks for their popularity. The sight is arresting. This box full of naked, plastic dolls confirms a secret knowledge. More than the mechanics of diapering, of mother-fathering, the "wet" babies are a silly joke, a diversion and a reassurance even, that the caretaker child or the passing voyeur is beyond such accidents, older, more experienced and infinitely more in control than these pitiful plastic babies heaped in a box like victims of some earthquake or holocaust.

GHOST BEACH

Swallows guard this beach, a crescent of shore. They swoop and arc in loops and spirals as if they were never absent or remiss.

Shadows flit between us, below the screech and caw of crows. In the dunes, long grasses befriend us. Stalks catch the breezes and wave welcome. My dress catches on the beach rose. I chew the tart, wild rosehip, spit out the fuzzy seeds. The marsh swarms with life.

Seasons revolve and we return to picnic. We inhabit the space we walk, the space we sit, the spaces in our eyes that tell each other, "*Yes. We exist for this moment.*"

Wooden stakes rise out of the water, symmetrical pilings in prearranged rows. Like an ancient monument of measurement, the posts stand weathered, erect and curious. The pilings catch the sun's journey from bay to pine-fringed ridge.

It's possible to measure days, years by the calculation of shadow. Who sank these smoothed and upright poles into the bay?

Did artists labor here, building this monument of logs? Who measured, sawed, honed the pilings, sinking each pole deep into the bed of this quiet water? There is a pattern to the rows. The image changes with the angle of sight.

On an afternoon such as this, the sea laps a calm. Mild, merciful winds brush out my hair. Birds never abandon this bay. We bring cups and thermos. The landscape is shaped by our presence. We wade out into the symmetry to join the pattern of upright poles.

Is the air treacherous? Is the water sinister? Or the woods? The broken piers, the cast-off cement, the gently lapping water, the deserted house. We know danger. One day in the year, we wander. We live for this day. What else is certain but time in this very moment. Moments, our eternity, we count them by the seasons. The sun witnesses our breath, our voices which mouth the words, "*Don't leave.*"

To mark our passing, to add something of ourselves, we bring long white ribbons. Unwinding streamers, we circle the poles, these tidemarks. We link what is not similar. We join what doesn't touch. Our knots please us. The precision of string, tied between poles. When we leave, ribbons circle the pilings; upright banners flutter from afar. We marvel at our handiwork, small tokens, potent gestures in a landscape of neglect, of abandonment. Seasons pass. Weather moves through memory like an apocalypse of the soul. The sober truth of impermanence.

In a year, when we return, the strands will be gone. Do the swallows take them for nests? The wind shares in the bounty. We will begin again. To circle what is dissimilar; to link separate entities; to picnic in the memory of our creations on this ghost of a beach.

A DESCENT INTO WINTER

Wild weather accompanies me like a perverse shadow. Not long after I move to California, the sky clouds over, catches on fire, and ash drifts down like fallout from Mount St. Helen's. I evacuate my home at the height of the Oakland hills firestorm.

I move one hundred miles north to a road named after a hot spring, an idyllic respite, I think, from the quake-prone, smog-shrouded Bay Area. But hot springs in active geothermal belts trigger side effects like sulfur clouds, condensed vapor, increased rainfall and earthquakes. Every week the tremors, clusters or swarms of them in Lake County, shake the wooden winterized summer home I rent until I'm sure the stone fireplace will crumble and the roof slide off the eaves.

Last summer I hit the road again. Looking back now, my itinerary included:

- Seeing my first tornado from the top of a great water slide at Water World, South Dakota,
- Hitting the first floods that swamped and devasted the Midwest when my car stalls in a huge puddle on a flooded street outside a bookshop in Iowa City,
- Arriving in the Hudson Valley of New York in time for a record heat wave: six torporific days of one hundred-degree weather and no air conditioning in my home - no electricity, for that matter. Then in the numbing midst of a sweltering ninety-four-degree afternoon, a torrential clattering of ice stones, hail the size of marbles!
- Witnessing the most severe winter in memory in upstate New York.

Going east from the Pacific coast, from the foothills of the Sierras right on across the country, temperatures drop far below those of the rain-forested West Coast. Northeast winters are familiar to every northeasterner, but this is my first winter where the snow stays on the ground longer than three days. I become an explorer in reverse, charting new personal territory. The permutations of water and ice; the delicacy of snow, the ardor of ice: charming and scary, awesome and treacherous. A country of snow in my backyard. I pull woolen clothes over silk skivvies, stock the cupboards with grains, dried beans, powdered milk and canned food to last a week in case my car can't plow out of the icy driveway.

The winter in Germantown, New York, begins late in the season. The last week of December the temperatures drop to the teens. An ice crust forms over rocks lining the banks of the creek that runs by the side of the converted barn where I live. The next day the ice crust covers the water where the creek disappears into shrubs out back, a path paved in ice. There is no sign of flowing water; the ice obliterates the very source of its existence. Under the bridge that crosses the road, the persistence of water prevails. A gurgle of air bubbles slips under the crust of ice. The bubbles struggle to pry loose. As the creek water level rises and falls during the day or night, so does the ice crust. Further downstream the crust is twelve inches deep.

My house is a quarter mile from the Hudson River. When I walk to the river I'm amazed to see a few drifting ice sheets. Thin, transparent, almost invisible, the ice floes drift south. I always thought floes were a sign of the spring thaw. In two days the entire river is frozen over. The immense Hudson under an ice sheet; I can hardly believe my eyes. Flowing water doesn't freeze. Yet, my eyes tell me differently. The river moves where I can't see. A few jutting ice holes. The rock I throw to test the thickness of the ice bounces. This is a first: to skip a flat rock on ice, instead of water. I count the bounces and try to improve my skipping technique. The rock skips along the ice fifty yards off shore and comes to an eerie stop.

Later when snow covers the ice, the river becomes a wide open field, frozen all the way across, a barren lunar wasteland. Icebreakers keep the channel near the western shore open. Tugs push barges through the jagged floes. Geese circle overhead, looking for open water. Deer, winter wanderers ever anxious to discover proverbial fields of plenty, gingerly step out on the ice. Is the grass greener across the river? They wonder, are the hunters' guns fewer?

I listen to the weather news when the first storm is predicted to hit the region. Snow is inevitable. I'm prepared, excited, and nervous. If the snow would just hurry up. I scan and rescan the cold, dull gray sky and wonder, will these thick clouds unleash the first flurries?

On the television a tsunami hits a Japanese coastal town; lava flows bury roads and homes in Hawaii; floodwaters swirl through living rooms in homes along the Mississippi River. There is some consolation in watching other people's weather. I forget the cold outside and remind myself that I'm safe. The disasters on the TV are the ones I missed.

Outside the snow falls silently and cautiously. I open the door, lift my hand to the sky and catch some flakes which instantly melt and vanish. Flake by flake, how innocuous the snow is when viewed up close in a palm. Pregnant clouds disguise their secrets. Vaporous water-laden air sheds, excretes and births multitudes of white flurries. The bravery of snow flakes: to bail out of a cloud in single file, to surrender to the fury and whim of the wind, and finally to collide and commingle. Flake embraces flake, the comradery of snow. The trickery of snow, to adhere, to coalesce to everything equally, a democracy of accumulations. The persistence of snow, masking rock, car, tree and pond. How gently snow amasses a quiet hold over everything that moves in any way but down.

I set a thermometer I bought at a garage sale in the window and check the outside temperature often: on rising, three or four times during the day, and before I retire at night. When the first snow flutters groundward, the anticipation is replaced by a new anxiety: how much will fall? How long will it snow; how bad will it be?

The snow falls so evenly the tall grasses aren't crushed but remain upright. On every tree branch facing north a three-inch topping.

One morning the temperature drops out of sight. When I bought the thermometer I didn't think about the range covered. The lowest demarcation of ten degrees seemed adequate. If it gets colder, I don't need to know how much colder, do I? Ten, five, zero, minus five . . . anything below thirty is cold to my western way of thinking. Now when the red line rests at the bulbous base next to the "made in USA," I know the temperature is zero or less.

After a month my cold tolerance increases: if the temperature is in the twenties I can walk the five blocks downhill to the Hudson River for ten minutes' gaze at the ice, the Catskills rising across the frozen water, then walk back. After forty-five minutes outside my thighs, covered with silk long johns under pants, grow red where the wind hits below my jacket. In the teens I can walk to the post office about three blocks away, but I bundle up my face and only breathe through a woolen scarf. Below ten degrees the outings are not pleasant; I only stay out for five minutes.

I walk to the river on a sunny morning before a storm. I stomp through ten inches of snow to get to the river bank. Snow the great equalizer—the Hudson River railway tracks—two parallel iron rails float on a white plain.

The river current pushed slabs of the icy crust up on the rocks creating ice ledges on shore which look like the giant steps of a mysterious ice stairway to the sky.

To warm my car motor I slog through snow, pull open the door and climb inside a car darkened by an eerie snow burial. The motor turns and catches. Outside I scrape off powdery snow with my glove before snow melts and refreezes to the windshield.

The mail deliverer won't service my box if the snow isn't cleared from around the post. In the summer I always walk to the post office. On a day in January when I try to walk the three blocks, my nose, concealed in a mohair scarf, stings in the cold wind. I turn back.

When the sun shines after a storm, I'm desperate to get out of the house. I walk the grounds of the school. An illuminated scene—the steel monkey bars, the geometric jungle gym, rising out of a clear white field of snow, casts long criss-crossing shadows. A fine layer of snow dusts each bar. When the snow blows off the school roof—snow smoke. The flakes are more granular than powdery, like glitter, tiny speckles of light. A maintenance man plows the basketball court but not the parking lot.

The kitten, like me, isn't used to snow. Together we gawk and stare; then make our way outside, cautious, curious and skeptical. The kitten puts a paw out to test the surface, then, not sure what to think but driven by a cabin fever equal to mine, she ventures a step. Quickly her paw slips through six inches of snow. Again she tries: paw tapping, stepping, falling through. She digs a hole in the snow, squats over the clearing, then buries the spot.

During all the winters of my life, rarely did the clouds shed snow. When they did, their outpouring was minimal, not effusive or wanton. Typically the snow manifested for a week, long enough to ice the roads and slick the sidewalks. I learned to look overhead when I walked under the snow-laden branches of pines. Snow people I rolled and molded with mittened hands stood guard on the front lawn. On the roof as snow capitulated under the dominance of the sun, a gurgling music resounded as the runoff fled the scene, a fast getaway. But like prison escapees who dash for freedom, the runoff's wild spree halted abruptly when the sun turned its back. Forced to suspend upside down from the roof, icicles shared an agonizingly slow and devious descent. Rarely did snow perform twice in a season; there were many seasons of abstinence.

With each new snowfall in this frigid season, my soul sinks lower into the ground in retreat from the sting and prick of ice. With each descent, however, that incorrigible optimist nears a new territory, a sunless land where heat nevertheless prevails in an intensity that outlasts the hottest summer. The coldest season is a soul-searching time. Indoors with my face to the double-paned window, I stare out as if I'm in an aquarium and remember other weather. A soul's memories include: the impermanence of the seasons; how one intensity replaces another; how to conjure faith to withstand fear and judgement; what to expect in the future.

I want to chart the evolution of the snowbank outside the front door but before the winter is a good month old, I've lost track; the cycle of snow falling, stacking, melting, refreezing and falling repeats over and over again.

Icicles on one Rhinebeck building drop five feet! One restaurant flaunts a jagged necklace of icicles all across the front gutter. Hanging from the outside stairs to the loft, glinting ice fangs.

No one uses tire chains. Plows come in many sizes: plows hooked to pick-ups, to 4 x 4's, to station wagons; city plow trucks, county plow trucks, highway plows emerging from dome-shaped snow huts off the interstate. The sanders are as heavy and sturdy as dump trucks. Mountains of rock salt and sand vanish before February. Three villages announce a snow emergency: all roads close until new sand and salt supplies are trucked in. During the coldest season in this recession, the economy booms at the salt mines.

My neighbor emerges after the first snow steering a tractor blower. The same machine that cuts his acre lawn in the summer, blows the maple and oak leaves in the fall, and now sucks up snow and spits out a ten-foot spray. The billowing white arches back away from the road.

To avoid spin-outs I go easy on the brakes. In the car I coast before a signal on a downhill stretch so I don't have to suddenly brake if the traffic light turns red. Likewise, if I'm headed uphill I don't want to stop midway so with my eye on the signal I creep upward, timing my arrival to carry me over the top of the hill on a green light.

There are few street lights in the county. At night I can't always see where a small country road leaves a larger state route. The fields and roads are one big blank snowy mass. Where are the divider reflectors that mark many California highways and the studded bumps set equidistant along a road's shoulder to jolt a driver awake if he or she strays off the road and onto the shoulder?

Before the biggest chill, where the temperature drops to minus twenty-eight, a friend reminds me to crack the water faucet. The pipes in the house weather zero degrees but if the temperature drops lower than minus ten the water inside the pipes freezes. At minus eighteen I put off reading the morning paper until noon since I don't want to trudge up the snowy driveway to get it until the temperature rises some.

Dressing to go outside takes ten minutes: long johns, outerwear, find and put on two gloves, two layers of wool socks, scarf, hat, then lace-up snow boots. I shovel snow from behind the car wheels so I can back out onto the plowed driveway. In the summer the long driveway looked secluded, private, alluring; now a long drive means lots of plowing and a long treacherous icy uphill climb. Not all ice shaves off the windshield with a scraper. Some tenacious ice, the remnant of an ice storm or freezing rain grips the windshield like cement. The defroster may take ten minutes to melt a ten-inch circular patch to see through. Ice also grips the headlights.

On the slate roof, a two-foot cover of snow turns to an icy menace. First some of the snow melts, then cold air refreezes the water; then the snow pack coalesces into a thick ominous ice sheet. Each day during a warm thaw the mass shifts downward. Out back one morning I hear a rumbling and run to the window just in time to see an avalanche. First the tremendous roaring overhead like someone rolling a heavy piano across the attic floor, then at the window a sheet of falling snow. Instantly a snow curtain crashes to the ground creating a six-foot snow mound. Out front the precipitous sheet doesn't fall, but dangles precariously. I watch the ice creep six inches a day, always closer to the ground. Each time I go out the door I run quickly to avoid a crashing mass. Five days later the ice ledge suspends three feet beyond the roof. Surely the force of gravity will suck down the overhang, I think. But I'm wrong. The treachery grows after more melting icicles dangle from the icy overhang secured to the roof by some invisible thread. This is how glaciers creep.

The neighbor circles her house and heads to her cellar. I call out, "Did your pipes freeze?" Why else head to the cellar, I think.

"My kitten ran away. She was just neutered and now she doesn't trust me." She held a bowl of food. "She thinks I brought the snow."

By early March, the fifteenth storm hits. The evergreens are pretty with the snow caught on their branches, pushing them earthward. The boughs seem dressed and trussed for holidays. On the morning after a big snow, without wind, every nook and cranny becomes a ledge: branches, the garbage can lid, the mail box, the chimney, the electric lines. The tiniest twig, the barren, twisting vines and the space between the window and the thermometer all bear a trace of white which twinkles in the rising sun.

Reading about other people's storms or the Los Angeles earthquake, which left thousands without homes, electricity or water calms me. Cold is relative. This is not the coldest place. At the post office a local man swears he'd never trade this weather with anyone: not for California's earthquakes, not for Iowa's floods or Florida's hurricanes. Snow is no big deal, he says. Build a fire if you get cold, or put on another sweater. I make pot after pot of hot, steaming barley broth soup and slip into mounds of hot, steamy, pine bath bubbles.

"This isn't cold," the cabbie in Manhattan tells me. "In Siberia it reached minus sixty degrees and my shoes were no good. That was the coldest. This is like Russian spring."

One night, a freezing rain clatters on the roof and wakes me. In the morning the consistency of the snow pack is glossy, like icing on a cake. Now a slick ice crust protects a layer of soft snow. The light-footed kitten walks on the thin crust but every two feet—the equivalent of eight kitten steps—a paw breaks through the surface and plunges down. Pat, pat, pat, pat, pat . . . plop! Pat, pat, pat, pat . . . plop!

When I walk to the mailbox the ice crust cracks and shatters under my feet. I enjoy the loud noise, the music of crunching steps. For a fraction of a second my boot balances on the ice crust, then crashes down through the three inches of soft snow underneath. The creak and moan of ice on the river like the silent growth of bones, the first cracks as the ice breaks up in the spring, the avalanching roof, the tinkle of tree ice falling on the ice crust . . . how to record these snow sounds?

The icy overhang finally crashes. The gutter where the ice pack stretched out into the air fattened under the weight of the glacial sheet.

The elderly woman who renovated the barn I live in became disoriented one winter day and locked herself out of the house. She broke a window but didn't have enough strength to climb in. She froze to death. Now I cringe whenever I notice the deep scratches on the front door. Were those hers? One woman, inspecting a leak in her basement, gets on her hands and knees and freezes to the floor. Her rescue is reported in the paper. After every big snow an elderly, over-ambitious snow shoveler suffers a heart attack. One man tries to loosen the snow covering his aluminum awning but dies when the snow buries him. Roofs weaken; heavy standing snow leaks into many homes. Metal pipes burst. Store roofs cave in, trapping shoppers. For plumbers, roofers, tow-truck drivers and insurance appraisers, a flurry of new business.

Everyone slips on the icy walks, driveways or roads. So far I'm lucky. My technique: walk very carefully, always keeping my body weight directly over the foot. This means if there is the slightest incline or decline, my body must compensate.

I'm sinking deeper and deeper into winter. The ice accumulates, changes and consumes the entire environment in ways I never imagined. Ice replenishes my drought-nourished, fire-numbed, quake-rattled imagination. I'm not alone in this cold Arctic fringe, not singled out for some freak punishment, some fluke of a disaster. Here we share the struggle equally, a communal survival effort. In the summer, on a stifling day, I'll reread these ice scenes and welcome a shiver.

Icy terrain vistas: on a rocky precipice when the ground snow melts, water begins to flow down the rocky surface like a waterfall. Midway down, however, the water refreezes into a lovely branching ice cascade. Some ground water seeps out of a crack in the rock, then ice whiskers and beards sprout directly out of the rock, as if from nowhere.

The snow reaches half way up my living room windows. Snow banks tower seven feet along the driveway. Some towns hire crews to shovel excess snow into dump trucks to haul away.

On the tracks a train whizzes past, vacuuming snow puffs into the air. The white smoky effect reminds me of cartoons where a character quickly runs away — only a little white cloud, indicating rapid departure, remains.

On the road a gusty wind lifts up powdery snow and blows the white granules like sand. Over the hill, rising tufts of snow. On the pavement swirling snow dust doesn't stick to the windshield or the pavement. At night, under a street light, soft, twirling snow reminds me of swarming summer insects attracted to the night light. I sneeze when a gentle flurry scatters feather-sized flakes, as if the old woman in the clouds just shook out her down comforter or pillowcase, setting the loose feathers afloat. Snow feathers never descend in a straight path, they climb, circle, loop and arc as if descent were an afterthought.

When ice falls from the branches along the driveway, the solid chunks clatter on the ice crust. A tinkling of falling icicles, then a silence as they come to a stop. On top of the icy crust, spilled ice jewels.

Last night reached a low low of minus twenty-seven degrees; I left the faucet dripping in the sink but forgot the bathtub so the cold water line froze up. After being snow bound three days, I was anxious to go outside even though the thermometer only read "made in USA" or zero. I dressed in two layers of silk skivvies, thermal double-layered socks, and hiking boots that gripped the ice. My plan: to get the car out on the road and go somewhere . . . to the grocery, the gas station, around the town loop—there are no blocks.

The driveway is a big obstacle. The gravel drive slopes uphill and my car wheels have a tendency to spin in place rather than grip the snow and climb up and out onto the plowed road. Once I get the car out, coasting back down the hill is easy. Getting out is the problem.

I enlist the help of a friend. I shovel the new snow from behind the tires, my friend wedges cardboard under the back wheels. I jump into the idling car, shift into reverse and . . . loud spinning. I repeat the process: lift more heavy, icy snow away from behind the car, chip at the ice there, then jam a harder flat piece of plywood under the tires. More spinning. Twenty minutes later the wheels still spin in place. Just as my fingers start to freeze up, the car spins out five feet and stops right smack in the middle of the driveway, blocking access to other cars.

We take a good look again up the icy hillish driveway. "If the car sticks here, there's no way it can climb that slope," I say. We reverse directions. With the same effort we used to get the car out of the parking space, we work to get the car back in. For a furious ten minutes we dig more snow, ram more plywood under the other side of the wheels. The tires spin. We rock the car and push with all our might to get the tires up and over uneven icy mounds. Then my friend slips and falls. He cusses and quits, leaving me holding the rear bumper. Immediately the car starts to slip backwards erasing our two feet of progress.

"The brake!" I shout. "Set the emergency brake."

After another five minutes I'm frozen and breathless but the car is back in place. When I get inside the house again, I feel relieved. I'm no longer restless, not totally defeated or resigned. My plan to get out worked . . . I just didn't get as far as I expected, no further than the driveway.

This is the lowest point of the season; my endurance is strained, tested. Not my endurance of the cold but of this unending oblivion, the boredom that comes with repetition. Snow is sneaky: I single out the flakes and marvel at the geometry of the six-pointed crystals, the inexhaustible, innocuous beauty, but when snow fraternizes and accumulates, large groups adopt a surly veneer, exude a stubborn and resistant streak. After the novelty of the ice vistas wanes, visual distractions do not compensate for the daily drudgery, the sluggish pace of tramping through snow, driving through snow, prodding cars, shopping carts, garbage cans through frozen slush. I crave greenery, water that flows and babbles idly, sun that warms the innermost cells of my being, a vine-ripened tomato, a wisteria-scented breeze.

Reckless with abandon, I vow to quit this longest, coldest, deepest, most icy season. When the first ground breaks through the icy cover, my eyes stare incredibly. After months of stepping on white snow pack, ordinary damp gravel appears colorful and fresh, like glistening sea rocks or polished stones. The vision is newfound and hallucinogenic. What undermines the deepest winter: anticipation, the suspense of new beginnings, the whisper of spring as the days lengthen; the breath of the wind mellows.

In early March friends in the West rave about their daffodils and blooming forsythia, but here another two inches of snow falls. I sulk. This is the time when faith in the afterlife of winter and faith in the resurrection of spring reassure me. The odds of surviving the coldest weather are easily in my favor. Winter is not a natural disaster but rather a drawn- out period of deprivation and hardship, of bitter cold and little sun.

Every phenomenon I witness—the changes in the weather and landscape; the birth and death of seasons, emotions and dreams—is ephemeral and shifty. I'd like to believe that a soul lives on after death, that a voiceless, bodiless soul attains a constancy and permanence that defies the natural laws of impermanence.

Weather moves through memory like an apocalypse of the soul, shaking my mind into acknowledging the sobering truth of impermanence. *Death may come at any time and quicker than a hurricane that heaves and howls for hours on end.* However I question the why of death, in the end I accept the truth of it. The body makes no claims to immortality. Death is inevitable, the final act of life.

Marilyn Stablein has lived in London, Kathmandu, Seattle, Houston and Berkeley. Her stories, essays and reviews have appeared in The Sun, ZYZZYVA, Fiction International and more than fifty other publications. Stories from her first book, *The Census Taker: Tales of a Traveler in India and Nepal,* won regional and national awards. She lives in New York's Hudson Valley.